MAKING SENSE OF THE ALT-RIGHT

MAKING SENSE OF THE ALT-RIGHT

GEORGE HAWLEY

COLUMBIA UNIVERSITY PRESS | NEW YORK

Columbia University Press

Publishers Since 1893

New York Chichester, West Sussex

cup.columbia.edu

Library of Congress Cataloging-in-Publication Data

A complete CIP record is available from the Library of Congress

ISBN 978-0-231-18512-7 (cloth : alk. paper)

ISBN 978-0-231-54600-3 (e-book)

Columbia University Press books are printed on permanent and durable acid-free paper.

Printed in the United States of America

Cover design: Noah Arlow

For Nina

CONTENTS

ACKNOWLEDGMENTS

I am grateful to the many patient and generous people who helped me complete this book. As always, I thank the University of Alabama for keeping me employed and allowing me the freedom to pursue my various research interests. I especially thank Joseph Smith, the chair of the political science department, who has been unfailingly supportive.

I owe a special thanks to Bridget Flannery-McCoy, my editor at Columbia University Press. Throughout this process, she has been helpful and encouraging. I have worked with many academic presses throughout my career but never before benefited from such a hands-on and hardworking editor. I am also grateful to my friend Jesse Merriam of Loyola University, who read an early draft of this manuscript and pointed out several of its blind spots.

This project has had more iterations than I care to count. When I began writing a follow-up to *Right-Wing Critics of American Conservatism* in early 2016, my original vision was very different from the final result. I initially planned something more ambitious, focused on what the Trump campaign taught us about the changing nature of the American right, with lengthy chapters on questions of economics, populism, demographics, and religion. I only planned to include a single chapter on the Alt-Right, and at the time I questioned whether it was even worth an entire chapter. Since then, of course, things have changed, and the need for a thorough scholarly examination of the Alt-Right became obvious. At Columbia University Press's request, I shelved (temporarily, I hope) the hundreds of pages I had already written on those other topics to focus on the Alt-Right specifically.

Because of this project's long journey, I must especially thank my wife, Kristen, who possesses a seemingly inexhaustible supply of patience and understanding. She has always been my most diligent copy editor and toughest critic. This year she perused more of my pages than ever before, sacrificing what little free time she has. I must also thank my three young children, Henry, Wyatt, and Nina. They are forever my most important source of motivation.

MAKING SENSE OF THE ALT-RIGHT

INTRODUCTION

The 2016 presidential election shattered assumptions about the normal rules of politics. We have come to expect a struggle between liberalism and conservatism in national politics; this time, that was not the case. Donald Trump ran to the left of Hillary Clinton on both trade and foreign policy, pushing for greater protectionism and a conciliatory attitude toward Russia, while simultaneously—and ostentatiously—running to the right of traditional Republicans on the issue of immigration. The Democrat, not the Republican, was accused of being too cozy with the financial industry and tyrannical governments in the Middle East. The leading voices of the organized conservative movement questioned whether they would support the GOP candidate. Some conservatives went so far as to endorse Hillary Clinton—a figure openly loathed by conservatives for at least two decades.

As Election Day approached, more oddities appeared. A month before Americans cast their ballots, mainstream commentators seriously asked whether the Democratic candidate could carry the deep red state of Utah, even though the race at the national level still looked fairly close.[1] Both candidates faced an unrelenting barrage of scandals, real or illusory.

WikiLeaks released thousands of hacked e-mails, some quite embarrassing, written by people associated with the Clintons. New allegations of sexual misconduct by Trump were released on a weekly basis, with counterallegations made about Clinton's husband. Clinton was cleared of any criminal wrongdoing in a scandal involving her e-mail server in July only to have the investigation reopened in the final stretch of the election; she was cleared again days later. Reasonable pollsters predicted a Clinton landslide on Election Day only to see Donald Trump win a stunning victory in the Electoral College—while simultaneously losing the popular vote by a significant margin.

Given everything that occurred in 2016, most observers can be forgiven for failing to note one additional bizarre moment when, in late August, Clinton experienced one of the weirdest examples of heckling in recent political history. As she was speaking, a lone voice shouted a single name: "Pepe!" The heckler was promptly escorted out, and the speech was not otherwise disrupted. I suspect few in the audience had any inkling what the "Pepe guy" was referencing.

Pepe is the name of an anthropomorphic cartoon frog. He originated on the now-defunct social-media website MySpace.[2] Pepe was part of a comic series known for its scatological humor; he was depicted urinating with his pants down his ankles and remarking, "Feels good, man." Over time, Pepe became popular as an Internet meme on sites such as 4chan.[3] He is frequently depicted hugging a similarly bizarre white-faced character known as "feels guy." In 2016, there was an entire page on Hillary Clinton's campaign website dedicated to Pepe.[4]

For reasons that are difficult to discern, Pepe became the mascot of the "Alt-Right," short for "alternative right." The

Alt-Right is, like Pepe, vulgar, irreverent, ironic, and goofy. Despite its innocuous name, the Alt-Right is also, at its core, a racist movement. I am generally hesitant (perhaps too hesitant) to label an individual, group, or political movement as racist. But in the case of the Alt-Right, there is no other appropriate word. I furthermore doubt that anyone seriously involved with the Alt-Right will challenge that characterization. Although mainstream conservatives and libertarians howl with outrage when they are labeled racists, the Alt-Right seems collectively to shrug its shoulders when it encounters this accusation. As one prominent figure on the Alt-Right put it, "We just don't care what you call us anymore."[5]

For this reason, some have objected that mainstream journalists and academics should not even use the term "Alt-Right" and should instead stick with "white supremacist."[6] Although I understand and appreciate this argument, throughout this text I will use the term "Alt-Right." At this point, the racist nature of the Alt-Right is well known, and it will be evident to the reader that I am not using the term to downplay this element of the movement. Relying exclusively on the umbrella term "white supremacist" would furthermore mask the ways the Alt-Right differs from other manifestations of the racial right. The Alt-Right is unlike any racist movement we have ever seen. It is atomized, amorphous, predominantly online, and mostly anonymous. Although it remains small, it is growing. And it was energized by Donald Trump's presidential campaign.

Understanding the Alt-Right is challenging for several reasons. It is a young movement both in the sense that it is new to the political scene and in the median age of its supporters. As such, it is still evolving. Although certain individuals are viewed as important figures in the Alt-Right, it is a movement without leaders, at least in the sense that most political movements have leaders. Both "cultural libertarians"—whose main complaint about contemporary America is the stifling degree of political correctness that shuts down discussion of important topics—and hardcore neo-Nazis have claimed the moniker of Alt-Right. In many respects, the Alt-Right is an outgrowth of Internet troll culture, which I will discuss in chapter 4. Scholars and journalists that reach out to the Alt-Right from a genuine desire to understand the movement can receive dishonest (or just baffling) answers.

The Alt-Right also poses a challenge for political observers who are used to thinking of politics in binary terms. Especially in the United States, with its two-party system, people tend to think in dichotomies: Republican versus Democrat, liberal versus conservative. Thus, whenever a new radical voice emerges on the political right, there is a tendency to describe it as a more extreme version of conservatism. In the case of the Alt-Right, this is inappropriate. Although diversity of opinion exists in the Alt-Right, it is not just a racist version of mainstream, *National Review*–style conservatism. The Alt-Right rejects the major premises of the conservative movement: the so-called three-legged stool of moral traditionalism, economic liberty, and strong national defense. None of these conservative shibboleths seem to interest the Alt-Right. If you follow any Alt-Right accounts on Twitter or visit the major Alt-Right websites, you will have a hard time finding anything about the Constitution, you will see no demands that liberals "support our troops," evangelical Christians are more likely to be mocked than defended, and bald eagles and American flags are few and far between. The Alt-Right is not just a new style of right-wing politics. It is totally distinct from conservatism as we know it. As the far-right activist Hunter

Wallace declared at the Southern nationalist website *Occidental Dissent*:

> In the United States, liberals, progressives, conservatives, and libertarians are all branches of the common liberal family. All these groups want to preserve the fundamental liberal world order even if they disagree on whether "liberty" or "equality" should be given priority and fight viciously with each other. They all share the same blinkered liberal worldview in which more "liberty" or more "equality" is the solution to every problem.
>
> We don't belong to the liberal family. We see ourselves as something else altogether. This is why, for example, so many of us enjoy trolling because we don't believe in any of the standard bullshit—for example, nothing is less self-evident to us than the notion that all men are created equal—and political correctness is an irresistible target.[7]

The Alt-Right is not just radical because it is racist—racism can be found in the ranks of many political ideologies. The Alt-Right's radicalism is also apparent in the degree to which it rejects other basic American values. Because it rejects both liberty and equality as ideals, it is difficult to compare the Alt-Right to most mainstream political movements. In spite of these challenges, it is possible to make sense of the Alt-Right while still acknowledging its internal inconsistencies and the chance that it will evolve and take new forms in the future. This is my task in this book.

I have a long-standing interest in right-wing movements, large and small, in the United States and abroad. In my previous book, *Right-Wing Critics of American Conservatism*, I argued that the mainstream conservative movement—a dominant force in American politics since the 1960s—is beginning to show its age and that it may soon face serious challenges from ideological opponents on the right. Conservatism's philosophical premises and bundle of policy proposals made political sense in the second half of the twentieth century. It is not clear they make sense any longer. The ground has shifted under conservatism's feet. The demographic base for conservative politics (white, married, middle-class Christians) is shrinking as a percentage of the electorate, and no conservative politician has yet found a way to reach out to new constituencies. The Cold War is over, and fear of communism is no longer sufficient to maintain a political coalition that always contained contradictory impulses—libertarians and moral traditionalists were always strange political bedfellows. Given these changes, there is little chance someone like Ronald Reagan will ever again occupy the White House.

While I recognized the waning of the conservative movement, I did not foresee the meteoric rise of the Alt-Right (although, as I will show, neither did the movement's founder). The American conservative movement and the Republican Party with which it is intertwined have been in chaos ever since Donald Trump kicked off his presidential campaign. But Trump could not have captured the GOP nomination if the mainstream right was not already in a weakened state. And the Alt-Right would similarly not be growing if more people continued to find traditional conservatism appealing.

Progressives, who have long viewed mainstream conservatives as their primary foe, may be delighted to see a fracturing of the conservative movement. Such a crack-up could very well usher in a new period of progressive hegemony in American politics. But that optimism should be tempered with caution. The mainstream conservative movement has long served as an important gatekeeper, keeping certain right-wing tendencies out of view and under control. Since the conservative movement emerged in the 1950s, it has engaged in periodic housecleaning—typically spearheaded by the late William F. Buckley, the founder of *National Review*. During these purges, the movement drove out open racists, anti-Semites, and conspiracy theorists from its ranks and from mainstream political discourse. If the mainstream right loses its legitimacy, all of its current supporters are not automatically going to become liberals. Following the breakdown of conservatism, new and destabilizing forces on the right are likely to emerge.[8]

The Alt-Right qualifies as such a destabilizing force. As a movement, it is both benefiting from the decline of traditional conservatism and working to expedite its final collapse. Although progressives have certainly been attacked by the Alt-Right, one can argue that the Alt-Right despises conservatives even more. Whereas earlier right-wing critics of the conservative movement wanted a seat at the conservative table, the Alt-Right wants to displace conservatism entirely and bring a new brand of right-wing politics into the mainstream.

As a warning to readers, I should note that much of the material presented in this book is unsettling. The existence of the Alt-Right and its large number of supporters and fellow travelers indicates that a "postracial America" is farther off than most people—liberal and conservative—have long hoped.

On a similar note, I was faced with a dilemma when determining what material to quote from figures from the Alt-Right. If I filled every chapter with the most shocking language that can be found within the Alt-Right, many people could reasonably accuse me of spreading its worst propaganda in an academic forum and of quoting terrible people who do not deserve to be noticed by anyone, and others could criticize me for cherry-picking the most disgusting remarks of the movement to damn everyone that supports it and for failing to examine its views impartially. On the other hand, if I only quoted the most reasonable and erudite supporters of the Alt-Right, I could be justly accused of whitewashing the most appalling aspects of the movement. Although there are downsides to both choices, I generally opted for the latter. For the most part, I chose to interview the more seemingly reasonable figures affiliated with the Alt-Right. In this short book, I rarely quote the worst examples of Alt-Right genocidal hatred and racial slurs. My primary focus is on those Alt-Right supporters who seek to appeal to ordinary Americans. This is because these are the elements of the Alt-Right that, in my estimation, are the most likely to influence American politics in the long run. But if anyone worries that I am denying the worst elements of the Alt-Right, let me say now that the most dreadful racial and religious insults are common among people who identify with this movement. The Southern Poverty Law Center, which has long monitored hate groups in the United States, describes the Alt-Right as an extremist ideology. I agree with that assessment.[9]

In spite of the potential pitfalls associated with doing so, in the pages ahead I will present this material as dispassionately as possible. If I paused to denounce every statement that I disagreed with, this would be a much longer book. Those looking for work that denounces the Alt-Right have many excellent options to choose from among mainstream voices across the political spectrum, from the *Weekly Standard* to *Mother Jones*.[10] My purpose here is to help readers understand the history, tactics, and possible future of the Alt-Right. To do this, I let the Alt-Right speak for itself, offering little of my own commentary; I trust most readers can reach their own conclusions without any opining from me. I do not think the Alt-Right's potential for future influence over American politics should be exaggerated. But I should also make clear that if the Alt-Right continues to grow in size, it may represent a serious challenge for America's liberal democracy, and for this reason it should be understood.

1

THE ALT-RIGHT'S GOALS AND PREDECESSORS

The Alt-Right can scarcely be called an organized movement. It has no formal institutions or a leadership caste issuing orders to loyal followers. There is no Alt-Right equivalent of *The Communist Manifesto*. Different people who describe themselves as part of the Alt-Right want different things. Using the loosest definition, we could say the Alt-Right includes anyone with right-wing sensibilities that rejects the mainstream conservative movement. But there are certain common, perhaps universal attitudes within the Alt-Right. The Alt-Right is fundamentally concerned with race. At its core, the Alt-Right is a white-nationalist movement, even if many (perhaps most) of the people who identify with the Alt-Right do not care for that term. The most energetic and significant figures of the movement want to see the creation of a white ethnostate in North America.

Because of its novel tactics, the Alt-Right represents something genuinely new on the American political scene. But it did not emerge from nowhere. We can see elements of the Alt-Right in preexisting movements, including mainstream conservatism. In this chapter, I will discuss some of the right-wing currents that made their way into the Alt-Right.

As I examine the Alt-Right's political and ideological genealogy, I must make one clarifying point. Although I see parallels between the Alt-Right and other right-wing movements in the United States, I am not suggesting that they are driven by the same underlying ideological premises. When I say that the Alt-Right, libertarianism, and conservatism have some features in common, I am not suggesting that either of those more mainstream ideologies share the racial animus and anxiety present in the Alt-Right.

Similarly, although there is a connection between the Alt-Right and earlier white-nationalist and white-supremacist groups, and some of those groups and their supporters have engaged in violence and terrorism, I am not implying that the Alt-Right is a terrorist movement. At the time of this writing, I am aware of no acts of physical violence directly connected to the Alt-Right—online harassment is another story, but I believe we should make a distinction between threatening tweets and real-world bombings, assaults, and murders. This is not to say that racist violence is not a real threat in contemporary America. We have, as just one example, the chilling case of Dylann Roof, who murdered nine parishioners at a historically black church in Charleston, South Carolina. Yet Roof's manifesto suggests he was more influenced by older white-nationalist writers and organizations, such as the Council of Conservative Citizens (the offspring of the Citizens Councils that once flourished in the South during and following the civil-rights era) and Harold Covington's Northwest Front, than by the Alt-Right.[1] It is possible that the Alt-Right will morph into something more dangerous and tangible in the real world,[2] and for that reason vigilance is necessary. But for now, the Alt-Right's activities are mostly limited to the Internet.

One more note on terminology before delving in: In the previous paragraph I used the terms "white nationalist" and "white supremacist." It is conventional among those that study the far right to label all racist groups "white supremacist." I do not oppose that convention. But it is worth noting that white supremacist is not usually the preferred term within the radical right. It instead relies on terms like "white nationalist," "white separatist," and "identitarian" (a word I will explain later). To outsiders, the distinction between a white supremacist and a white nationalist may not be obvious. But activists on the radical right claim there is an important difference. According to far-right nomenclature, a white supremacist favors a society in which people of multiple racial backgrounds live together but where whites are the socially dominant group (as in the Jim Crow South or apartheid South Africa). In contrast, a white nationalist favors the complete separation of the races into separate states. Many white nationalists also deny that their vision is based upon the belief that whites are a superior race. As a white nationalist who used the penname Ygdrasil put it, "The desire of White Nationalists to form their own nation has nothing to do with superiority or inferiority."[3] The sincerity of such statements is, at best, questionable, as open hostility toward other races is common within far-right movements.

Throughout this text, I use the term "white nationalist" largely because that is the term used by many on the Alt-Right to describe themselves. But I acknowledge the critique that white nationalism was a term invented to make white-supremacist views more palatable.

WHAT DOES THE ALT-RIGHT WANT?

There are diverse opinions within the Alt-Right. In fact, as I will show in the conclusion, it appears that this diversity is increasing. But the core of the Alt-Right remains white identity, even if many of the people who now associate with the Alt-Right do not call themselves white nationalists. So what does white identity really mean in terms of policy? At present, the Alt-Right is not unified on this question.

The neo-Nazi element of the Alt-Right desires the creation of something akin to the Third Reich, with everything this entails. Their best-known website is the *Daily Stormer*, run by a neo-Nazi named Andrew Anglin. Sites like this are where you find the most outrageous and violent rhetoric, delivered without a hint of irony. At the *Daily Stormer*, articles with titles like "Jew Admits Dreams of Defiling Aryan Blood" are common.[4] The openly neo-Nazi are the most extreme element of the Alt-Right, and this facet of the Alt-Right is similar to the older varieties of white nationalism in the United States. Neo-Nazis are also frequently denounced by others associated with the Alt-Right on the grounds that they taint the movement's "brand."[5] The most flamboyant neo-Nazis are even accused by others on the Alt-Right of being "FBI informers and [Anti-Defamation League] shills," deliberately harming the movement.[6]

The neo-Nazi wing of the Alt-Right, which does not seek to distance itself from the Holocaust and talk of race wars, appears to be in the minority. Others on the Alt-Right tend to eschew the most extreme rhetoric while still calling for the creation of an all-white country or something very close to it. Yet few people in the less radical corners of the Alt-Right have explained in any detail how this can be achieved.

This is one way that the Alt-Right tends to differ from earlier white-nationalist movements. People like William Pierce and Harold Covington were quite explicit when explaining how whites would reclaim all or part of the world. In his 1978 novel *The Turner Diaries,* Pierce described a global race war, instigated by a small circle of elites, which ultimately led to apocalyptic levels of violence, including the use of nuclear weapons around the globe. Harold Covington's vision was less ambitious, but his novels about the creation of a white nation in the Pacific Northwest also involved extreme violence—in Covington's imagination, the war would be won by tactics developed by the Irish Republican Army in the twentieth century. On the most visible platforms of the Alt-Right, such calls for revolutionary violence are uncommon.

Richard Spencer (who is the person most associated with the Alt-Right and who will be discussed in detail in the coming chapters) supports the idea of creating one or more white ethnostates in North America. While he does not seem to anticipate some kind of violent conflict as the major catalyst for the creation of such an ethnostate, he also admits he does not have a clear idea about how such a state will come about. Spencer told me: "I don't know how we're going to get there, because the thing is, history will decide that for us. History has lots of twists and turns. . . . You have to wait for a revolutionary opportunity to present itself, and history will present that opportunity."[7] According to Spencer, the idea of a white ethnostate is now akin to Zionism at its early stages: "We need to go back and look at [Zionism's] most basic impulses. And its basic impulses are identitarian."[8] At this stage, much of the Alt-Right will be happy if they simply plant the idea of white nationalism in the minds of people who had never previously been open to the notion—the exact policies can apparently be worked out later.

Some writers on the Alt-Right have offered more specific details about how a white-nationalist vision can be achieved without resorting to a brutal race war. According to Greg Johnson (also prominent in the movement and the subject of more discussion shortly): "If it was not too much trouble for all these people to come here, then it will not be too much trouble for them to go back."[9] He suggested that if white nationalists become a dominant force in American politics, it will be fairly straightforward to implement policies that encourage nonwhites to leave the country. He did acknowledge, however, that after the easier steps are taken—such as the deportation of undocumented immigrants—more draconian measures will need to be implemented.[10]

Among the less radical voices within the Alt-Right, the long-term goal seems to be more modest: an end to mass immigration, the end of political correctness, and the acceptance of white identity politics as a normal element of mainstream politics. Rather than the destruction of the United States as it is currently constituted and the creation of a new white nation, some say that they will be satisfied if whites simply stop shrinking as a percentage of the population. As one Alt-Right supporter on Twitter told me: "The majority of alt-righters do not think the goal of an all-white nation is realistic. They just want to stop the bleeding."[11] Within the Alt-Right, commentary on race ranges from calls for massive ethnic cleansing, through violent means if necessary, to new restrictions on nonwhite immigration into the United States. But even the mildest elements of the Alt-Right are far to the right of mainstream conservatives, and all agree that race is the movement's single most important issue.

Outside of the race question, there are a few other points of agreement, although exact policy positions are often lacking. We can say that the Alt-Right is also an antifeminist movement opposed to contemporary notions of gender equality and in favor of a more patriarchal society. But its critique of feminism is not usually based on traditional religious arguments about gender roles. The Alt-Right promotes what it calls "sex realism"—that men and women have biological differences that make them suited to different social roles. There is some overlap between the Alt-Right and the so-called Men's Rights Movement, which argues that discrimination against men is now a greater problem than discrimination against women.

The Alt-Right also uniformly rejects traditional Republican views on foreign policy. I am aware of no one on the Alt-Right who supports Bush-era strategies for the War on Terror, for example. The Alt-Right, for the most part, has favorable attitudes toward Vladimir Putin of Russia and Bashar al-Assad of Syria. It has no interest in spreading democracy abroad and opposes the close relationship between the United States and Israel. But, again, there is not a specific Alt-Right foreign-policy platform.

On other policy issues, there are few points of universal agreement. Unlike mainstream conservatism, the Alt-Right does not have much to say about economics. Broadly speaking, few on the Alt-Right favor the kind of laissez-faire economic policies traditionally promoted by conservatives and libertarians, and most seemed to favor Donald Trump's call for new economic protectionist measures. But the proper level of taxation and economic regulation seem to be peripheral issues for the Alt-Right. The movement is also divided on issues such as tolerance for homosexuals and abortion, but these issues (so important to many conservatives) do not interest the Alt-Right very much.

For the Alt-Right, identity politics is everything. Conservatives say that they are fundamentally interested in ideas—constitutional government, liberty, morality, etc. They furthermore argue that these ideas are universal and equally accessible to all people. For this reason, conservatives often declare that they have no problem with nonwhite immigration, provided the newcomers assimilate to American values. In contrast, the Alt-Right views the world as being fundamentally divided into competing groups, and the success of their group (whites) is their primary concern. If a core conservative principle such as individual liberty is a hindrance to their group's collective interests, then that principle can and should be jettisoned. Thus, to the Alt-Right, constitutional questions about equality are beside the point. If the Constitution dictates a policy that is inimical to white interests, then the Constitution is the problem.

WHAT DOES THE ALT-RIGHT DO?

The Alt-Right is almost exclusively an online phenomenon. It has no brick-and-mortar think tanks distributing policy papers to congressional staffers. It does not run any print newspapers, have a meaningful presence on television, or broadcast its message on the radio. No major politician or mainstream pundit is a self-described Alt-Right supporter. It is predominantly anonymous. For all of these reasons, it is remarkable that it became such a visible presence in American politics in 2016.

The Alt-Right is able to punch above its weight in the political arena because it is very good at using the Internet. Like other ideological movements, the Alt-Right has a large number of blogs, podcasts, forums, and webzines that discuss cultural and political ideas—examples of these include *Radix*, *The Right Stuff*, *Counter-Currents*, *American Renaissance*, and many others. The Alt-Right's primary activity during its initial phase, which roughly lasted from 2008 until 2013 and which I will discuss further in the next chapter, was the publication of short essays at infrequently visited websites.

Starting in about 2015, however, the Alt-Right began embracing new tactics, although writers on the Alt-Right continued to generate essays at various websites. It now also has a constellation of online message boards, such as /pol/, My Posting Career, and Salo Forum, where the radical right gathers anonymously and shares ideas and new content. There are also private forums that require a username and password to access. Each of these forums has its own style and rules, and many of the most memorable Alt-Right memes seem to have originated at these sites. But even in its use of message boards, the Alt-Right is not especially different from the older white-nationalist movement. Stormfront, a white-nationalist message board with the motto "White Pride Worldwide," has been in operation since the mid-1990s. The ability to break out of these isolated Internet ghettos and enter the mainstream discussion is what sets the Alt-Right apart from its predecessors.

The Alt-Right successfully injected itself into the national conversation when it mastered the art of trolling. An Internet troll is someone who fosters discord online, provoking strong emotional reactions from readers and often changing the topic of conversation. Trolling does not always have an obvious political purpose; a troll may be looking for nothing but a moment of nihilistic amusement. Trolling can take the form of insulting someone's appearance or deliberately giving bad advice about a technological problem, for example. But the Alt-Right trolls for a purpose. By leaving sites specifically aimed at a radical right-wing audience and joining discussions at other message boards, in, for example, the comment sections of major news venues, YouTube, and especially on Twitter, the Alt-Right is able to circulate its message widely. Alt-Right trolls help disperse the movement's views far beyond what would be possible if the movement could only be found on its own platforms. I will discuss this in greater detail in chapter 4.

The use of irony and humor is another Alt-Right innovation. The Alt-Right presents itself as a fun movement, one using Internet jargon familiar to tech-savvy millennials and eager to needle established journalists, academics, celebrities, and politicians. Whereas older white nationalists came across as bitter, reactionary, and antisocial, much of the Alt-Right comes across as youthful, light-hearted, and jovial—even as it says the most abhorrent things about racial and religious minorities.

Although the Alt-Right mainly exists online, the movement does now have some formal and informal gatherings in the real world. The National Policy Institute hosts regular conferences where Alt-Right supporters listen to speeches about race, immigration, and other political topics and meet face to face. American Renaissance has long hosted similar conferences, which started to attract members of the Alt-Right as the movement grew. These formal gatherings have a limited audience because they force supporters of the Alt-Right to shed their anonymity. People willing to post racist material under a pseudonym online may not be willing to walk through a crowd of protesters and journalists to listen to a white-nationalist speaker. But the Alt-Right does seem to have a growing number of informal meetups, not publicly advertised, where the movement's followers can gather privately. There are now guides online about how these kinds of gatherings can be organized.[12]

PREDECESSORS

Although the Alt-Right is a new movement, it has many ideological forebears. It shares some similarities with mainstream conservatism, with libertarianism, and especially with paleoconservatism. The most obvious precursors to the Alt-Right were the older white-nationalist movements in the United States, which must first be understood if we wish to know why the Alt-Right is unique.

TRADITIONAL WHITE NATIONALISM

Detailing the history of white nationalism in America is trickier than it first appears. This is because, despite the egalitarian rhetoric of the Declaration of Independence, the United States operated as a de facto white-supremacist nation for most of its history. This has been a subject of controversy for decades. No one disputes that slavery poses a problem for the narrative that America is, and always was, a beacon for freedom and equality. But debates continue as to what the most important Founding Fathers "really" thought about race and the future of equality. Many historians, especially contemporary conservative historians, are inclined to view the marquee names of the American Revolution as opponents of slavery who made an immoral choice—allowing slavery to continue—

for the sake of keeping the union together. There is no doubt that Thomas Jefferson, among others, was convinced that slavery could not and should not persist in the United States, at least in the long term. Yet even if we view Jefferson's statements on this subject as sincere, it is equally clear that Jefferson was no racial egalitarian—see his "Notes on the State of Virginia," where he states his belief that blacks "are inferior to the whites in the endowments both of body and mind."[13] The case against Jefferson as an egalitarian is even weaker when we note that Jefferson hoped that, after slavery was eventually abolished, freed blacks would be returned to Africa.[14]

Moving forward through history, it is easy to find evidence that Americans continued to view the United States as a "white country," and policies designed to maintain white demographic dominance were often uncontroversial: the Chinese Exclusionary Act of 1882, the Immigration Act of 1924 (which ushered in a four-decade period of low immigration), and President Eisenhower's Operation Wetback (which forcibly deported undocumented immigrants), to name just a few. The Progressive movement that thrived in the early twentieth century had a transparent racial and eugenicist element to it. Famous progressive eugenicists such as Madison Grant and Lothrop Stoddard thought the idea of racial equality was absurd. The United States began to change course on issues of race following World War II, eventually abolishing racial segregation, allowing large-scale immigration from non-European countries, and later electing an African American president. But white supremacy was formally institutionalized throughout most of American history.

On this point, many of today's white nationalists and contemporary progressives agree. Conservatives frequently argue that America's founders had a sincere vision of equality and that they pointed the way toward a peaceful, diverse, and egalitarian society. But this narrative is commonly rejected today by both white nationalists and progressives. Jared Taylor, of the "race-realist" group American Renaissance, probably agrees with Senator Bernie Sanders on very little, but his own writings on this subject ("Since early colonial times, and until just a few decades ago, virtually all Whites believed race was a fundamental aspect of individual and group identity")[15] clearly echo Sanders's claim that the United States was created "on racist principles."[16] Although they reach different conclusions, both men argue that the United States was viewed by its founders as a country for people of European ancestry.

For all of these reasons, it is important to disaggregate those groups and individuals throughout American history that were white nationalist and white supremacist in a general sense—that is, they accepted the views on race that were common at the time—from those that treated race as their primary concern. When thinking about the history of white racial movements in the United States, the first group that typically comes to mind is the Ku Klux Klan, which formed in the South during the Reconstruction era, though it faded from prominence after just a few years. The Klan experienced new growth, in both the North and South, following the release of the 1915 film *The Birth of a Nation*, which valorized the group. This new iteration of the Klan similarly receded from the public eye over the following decade. The Klan saw another resurgence during the civil-rights era, engaging in a number of terrorist acts. Its membership ranks dwindled again after that, and by 2016 it had nothing resembling a centralized leadership, and just a handful of small, disorganized groups continue to use the name.[17] Nonetheless, the Klan left a deep imprint on America's consciousness and even today remains salient in the public imagination. Donald Trump's opponents, for example, were eager to promote evidence that he had enthusiastic support from the KKK.[18]

Besides the Klan, other white racial groups arose in the United States in the latter decades of the twentieth century. Most of these are now in a similar state of disarray or no longer exist. George Lincoln Rockwell formed the American Nazi Party in 1959. This party never won an election and quickly fell apart after Rockwell's murder by a colleague in 1967. William Pierce founded the white-nationalist National Alliance in 1974. It had a longer run than similar organizations but was also unable to maintain any significance following the death of its founder in 2002—though the National Alliance does now have a new website. Aryan Nations, led by Richard Butler, was also formed in the 1970s, but a 2000 lawsuit dealt the group a devastating blow from which it never recovered.

All of these groups may be considered precursors to the Alt-Right in the sense that they advocated white nationalism, but the overlap (an obviously significant overlap) largely ends there. Irony and humor—essential to the Alt-Right—were all but nonexistent in these earlier movements. Alt-Right material often has a sense of amused detachment, something not present in any of William Pierce's radio broadcasts. In contrast to the Alt-Right on Twitter, I doubt that anyone who visited the Aryan Nations compound was left wondering whether the people they met genuinely believed what they said or if they were just "trolling" because they found it funny.

The issue of tone is important. Rage and hate were the primary emotions associated with the older white-nationalist movement. Even when it dabbled in popular culture, such as with the record label Resistance Records (which released punk and heavy-metal albums with white-nationalist lyrics), it was a movement transparently driven by resentment. No one could read *The Turner Diaries* without being convinced that William Pierce literally wanted to see nonwhites exterminated. The Alt-Right offers something more attractive to potential supporters: edginess and fun. Someone who would never associate with a group like the Klan or the National Socialist Movement might eagerly watch YouTube videos by the Alt-Right satirist RamZPaul. This is a curious paradox of the Alt-Right; it may ultimately be a greater threat to mainstream politics than these earlier groups precisely because it often comes across as much less threatening.

To take just one example: When an article about a university contest for Holocaust art was published online, Alt-Right trolls immediately began posting in the article's comment section, relaying absurd stories about their families' experiences in concentration camps. One of these comments stated, "All six of my grandmothers were survivors. They avoided being gassed by playing alto saxophone and electric piano solos for the guards while hiding in a pile of rubble."[19] Whereas earlier white-nationalist movements often claimed the Holocaust never happened, the Alt-Right typically treats it as a joke.

Also unlike the Alt-Right, these older groups were real organizations with actual members and formal leaders. Although their membership lists were private, they did exist, and people joined using their real names. Because they were real-world organizations, the older white-nationalist groups in America could make their presence known in their communities. The actual leaders of these movements, who could plausibly claim to speak for their members, could be identified. Yet by being real organizations, they were limited in their ability to grow, especially as tolerance toward open racists in the United States began to decline. For the Alt-Right, anonymity and atomization can be viewed as a strength. People can say things anonymously on the Internet that they would never utter on the streets. And if someone disagrees with another voice of the Alt-Right, even a supposed leader, he or she cannot be kicked out of the movement. Yet there are also limits to what a mostly online movement can accomplish. Even if the Alt-Right came to dominate social media completely (which is unlikely), it is an open question as to how effectively it could translate that into real-world political victories.

In terms of strategy and tactics, the Alt-Right shares little with the most frightening white-nationalist organizations of the twentieth century. But history has seen another approach to American white nationalism, a side that is more directly connected to the Alt-Right. For lack of a better term, I call it "highbrow white nationalism."

Avoiding the violence and pageantry of the Klan and various neo-Nazi groups, the highbrow white-nationalist movement, complete with quasi-scholarly journals, books, and websites, has been around for decades. This variety of white nationalism presents itself as a movement of serious scholars and social observers—including many people with impeccable academic credentials. The people associated with this variety of white nationalism tend to maintain a civil tone, avoiding the racial slurs, threatening language, and vitriol for which groups like the KKK and skinhead gangs are known.

Jared Taylor, whom I briefly introduced above, is the leading figure of this variety of white nationalism, though he eschews the term. Taylor has been a prominent voice in this movement since the early 1990s, when he created the New Century Foundation, best known for its publication *American Renaissance* and its conference of the same name.[20] He presents arguments in favor of what he calls "race realism."

Among highbrow white nationalists, there has long been a fascination with and promotion of what the blogger Steve Sailer (who is not a white nationalist) calls "human biodiversity," typically shortened to HBD. In contrast to the position advanced by mainstream contemporary academics, this perspective holds that racial and ethnic distinctions are rooted in biology, rather than being mere social constructs. This is what Taylor means when he refers to race realism. According to this view, social disparities between racial and ethnic groups are going to persist, regardless of any efforts to create a more equitable society. And because efforts to reverse generations of social injustice and create an equal society are doomed to fail, they should not even be attempted; instead, racial differences should be calmly accepted as a reality, with the corollary belief that different racial groups should separate from one another—ideally into separate ethnostates.

For a time, Taylor had access to large media venues. Taylor's first book on race, *Paved with Good Intentions*, was released by a major publisher in 1992.[21] Early American Renaissance conferences were televised on CSPAN. By the late 1990s, however, Taylor was largely absent from the public eye, remaining known mostly by the people who subscribed to his magazine or read his website, as well as by people working for organizations that monitor hate groups.

But as the Alt-Right movement took off, Taylor became a revered figure. His American Renaissance conferences now are a major meeting place for the Alt-Right. But he is not completely uncontroversial in Alt-Right circles. Taylor has always carefully avoided anti-Semitism, as even groups such as the Southern Poverty Law Center acknowledge.[22] This makes him problematic to the most anti-Semitic elements of the

Alt-Right, who, like the Nazis before them, view the so-called Jewish Question as their most important issue.

Although Taylor may be the best-known proponent of highbrow white nationalism, a few others are worth mentioning. Kevin MacDonald, unlike Taylor, is a beloved figure among contemporary anti-Semites. He is best known for his books on Jews: *A People That Shall Dwell Alone*, *Separation and Its Discontents*, and *A Culture of Critique*.[23] MacDonald, a retired professor of psychology who spent most of his career at California State University–Long Beach, argued that Judaism is more than a religion or ethnicity; it is instead a "group evolutionary strategy" that encourages Diaspora Jews to undermine the power of majority groups. The people in the Alt-Right that are eager to identify which of their enemies are Jewish follow a tactic developed by MacDonald in his books, especially *A Culture of Critique*. In that work, MacDonald documented the degree to which Jews were overrepresented in efforts to liberalize immigration policies and undermine white-supremacist policies. MacDonald now edits the white-nationalist webzine *The Occidental Observer*.

Greg Johnson is another highbrow white nationalist whose work began before the Alt-Right existed. Johnson, who has a Ph.D. in philosophy, first became publicly involved in white nationalism in 2007, when he began editing the *Occidental Quarterly*—a print journal that follows a format similar to a mainstream scholarly journal.[24] Johnson began his own venture in 2010, when he created the webzine *Counter-Currents*, which has pushed for the creation of a "North American New Right" (modeled largely on the European New Right)[25] and "is a White Nationalist metapolitical movement that seeks to lay the foundations of a White Republic or republics in North America."[26]

As was the case with more outlandish and threatening white-nationalist organizations, few would view highbrow white nationalism as a "fun" movement. Just as calls for terrorism and violent revolution have a limited appeal, the number of people who care to read dry, repetitive discussions of IQ distributions or look at charts comparing crime rates by race is also probably small. However, the more intellectual figures on the Alt-Right are clearly well versed in these works. And today, highbrow white nationalism can be considered part of the larger Alt-Right family.

PALEOCONSERVATISM

Paleoconservatism is now an exhausted force in American politics. However, for some time it represented the most serious right-wing threat to the mainstream conservative movement. Paleoconservatism first emerged in the 1980s, largely as a response to the rising influence of neoconservatism.[27] Neoconservatives came to prominence within the conservative movement in the 1970s; many of the first neoconservatives were former leftists. Their views on issues such as race and the welfare state tended to be more moderate than those of earlier conservatives, and their views on foreign policy were typically quite hawkish. Neoconservatives were largely responsible for the shift in the conservative movement as a whole (as well as the Republican Party) to more ideological, militaristic, and egalitarian positions. The paleoconservatives—who, unlike the Alt-Right, still saw merit in the conservative project—pushed back against this, arguing that conservatism had lost its way and needed to be reformed.[28] The paleoconservatives represented an older form of conservatism, one skeptical of American intervention abroad, willing to support tariffs and other forms of protectionism, and openly opposed to state-sponsored efforts to promote racial equality.

In the early 1980s, the neoconservatives and paleoconservatives uneasily coexisted under the big tent that was the conservative movement, but by the mid-1980s, it was clear that one of the two groups would have to go. They disagreed on too much to collaborate in any meaningful way. And once that battle started, there was little doubt which camp would emerge victorious—the neoconservatives were much better funded and more media savvy. Although it had little substantive effect on public policy, a pivotal moment came in the struggle over who Ronald Reagan would appoint as the chair of the National Endowment for Humanities (NEH). Reagan's initial pick was M. E. "Mel" Bradford, who approached politics and culture from a paleoconservative perspective. Bradford clearly had the proper academic credentials for the position (a Ph.D. from Vanderbilt, multiple academic positions, and a large stack of books bearing his name), but his views were controversial at a time when conservatism was trying to distance itself from its recent, more openly racist past. In his writings, Bradford had defended the Confederacy and the social institutions of the South more generally, and he rejected the notion that greater equality should be an important political goal.[29]

Although chairman of the NEH was a modest position, others in the conservative movement were appalled that Reagan would consider such a person for any leading role in a federal agency. Conservatives such as Irving Kristol preferred the less radical—but less accomplished—William Bennett. The decisive moment apparently came when William F. Buckley got involved in the dispute, backing Bennett.[30] Reagan subsequently withdrew Bradford from consideration. This was the first clear sign that the paleoconservatives were going to be marginalized, if not expelled, from mainstream conservatism entirely.

As the Alt-Right did with Trump, the paleoconservatives put their hopes in a presidential candidate. In the paleoconservative case, Patrick J. Buchanan represented the best chance to conquer the Republican Party and dethrone the neoconservatives as the leaders of the mainstream American right. Buchanan, a former staffer for both Nixon and Reagan, had impressive conservative and Republican credentials. But he disagreed with the new direction of the conservative movement. In 1992 and 1996, he mounted populist campaigns in the GOP presidential primaries, running on a platform of economic protectionism, immigration restrictionism, foreign-policy noninterventionism, and cultural traditionalism. He never came close to securing the nomination—though he did win the important New Hampshire primary in 1996—but he did cause considerable concern among leading figures of the conservative movement. Buchanan's rhetoric about America's relationship with Israel was considered particularly problematic, with many conservatives arguing that Buchanan had crossed the line between reasonable criticism of Israeli policies and outright anti-Semitism—*National Review* dedicated an entire issue to just this subject. (In early 2016, *National Review* also dedicated an entire issue to denouncing Donald Trump.)

But while the paleoconservatives were like the Alt-Right in their hostility toward the conservative movement, they sought to change conservatism, not destroy it. Although I will not go so far as to label the entire paleoconservative movement as racist, it is true that most paleoconservatives were more comfortable talking about issues like immigration in explicitly ethnic terms. One of Pat Buchanan's most recent books, for example, included a chapter titled "The End of White America."[31]

What little remains of the paleoconservative movement does not seem to have much interest in the Alt-Right. One point of contention is religion. The paleoconservatives were almost all religious traditionalists, whereas the Alt-Right has a decidedly secular (and sometimes anti-Christian) orientation. The paleoconservative magazine *Chronicles* has never, to my knowledge, published anyone directly connected to the Alt-Right since the movement appeared on the scene.

There are only two people from the paleoconservative movement associated with the Alt-Right in any meaningful way. The first is Paul Gottfried, a well-known critic of neoconservatism. I do not classify Gottfried as part of the Alt-Right. Gottfried, who is Jewish, is not an anti-Semite, and he rejects white nationalism. But Gottfried's scholarly work certainly influenced many people on the Alt-Right—especially his books and columns critiquing the conservative movement. He also seems to have been something of a mentor to Richard Spencer, who coined the term "Alt-Right," and he wrote articles for both *Taki's Magazine* and *Alternative Right*, where the term was first popularized.

The second, Sam Francis, was in my view the paleoconservative whose ideas had the greatest influence on the Alt-Right—though he died in 2005, well before the Alt-Right concept was born. Of the major paleoconservatives, Francis was the most openly racist. For much of his career, he held important positions within the conservative movement; he served on a senator's staff, he worked for the Heritage Foundation, and held an editorial position at the *Washington Times*. His willingness to cross the line into open racism was the reason he ultimately became unwelcome in the mainstream conservative movement. Francis was also closer to the Alt-Right and farther from most paleoconservatives in that he was not particularly religious.

RADICAL LIBERTARIANISM

On its face, libertarianism seems like it would be in fundamental, philosophical opposition to the Alt-Right. Libertarianism is an individualist ideology hostile to all forms of identity politics, including racial identity politics. It is true that libertarian principles preclude state-directed efforts to promote racial equality, but influential libertarian thinkers including Milton Friedman have argued that their preferred policies would actually lead to a more racially tolerant and equal society.[32]

The typical libertarian argument about race goes something like the following: yes, government regulations forcing business owners to serve or hire people they would prefer not to serve or hire (including racial, ethnic, and religious minorities) represent violations of the nonaggression principle[33] and thus should be opposed on libertarian grounds. However, money does not see color. Therefore, a business that makes decisions based on noneconomic characteristics (such as race or religion) will be less efficient than one that does not hold these irrational prejudices. Over time, the free market will reward those that refuse to discriminate and drive others out of business. In the long run, according to the mainstream libertarian view, unfettered capitalism is the best solution to racial tensions.

However, within libertarianism there are figures that are less optimistic about the future of race relations, even in a society with limited (or no) government. Murray Rothbard, a well-known libertarian economist who joined paleoconservatives in supporting Buchanan in his presidential run, was perhaps the most significant of these. Although Rothbard was a principled libertarian, he was also an antiegalitarian. He wrote an essay titled "Egalitarianism as a Revolt Against Nature," in which he argued that equality is "impossible in view of the physical nature of man and the universe."[34] Rothbard also defended *The Bell Curve*, a controversial book by Charles Murray (also a libertarian), which argued that economic inequality in the United States could be partially explained by genetic differences in intelligence.[35]

Hans-Hermann Hoppe may be the most important bridge between libertarianism and the Alt-Right. His most famous book, *Democracy: The God That Failed*, argued that democracy is a suboptimal form of government, one inclined toward short-sighted thinking; according to Hoppe, if you insist on having a government, it should be a monarchy.[36] Hoppe has also condemned mass immigration as not being the result of free choices of individuals but actually an example of "forced integration."[37] Other libertarians continue to lambast liberal immigration policies on the grounds that they tend to strengthen the state in the long run. Lew Rockwell, the president of the Ludwig von Mises Institute, recently made this argument:

> It is impossible to believe that the U.S. or Europe will be a freer place after several more decades of uninterrupted mass immigration. Given the immigration patterns that the US and EU governments encourage, the long-term result will be to make the constituencies for continued government growth so large as to be practically unstop-

pable. Open-borders libertarians active at that time will scratch their heads and claim not to understand why their promotion of free markets is having so little success. Everybody else will know the answer.[38]

While a direct ideological connection between libertarianism and the Alt-Right is tenuous at best, the above statements overlap with many Alt-Right arguments, and many of the major figures on the Alt-Right at one point considered themselves libertarians. This seems to be especially true of the writers associated with the Alt-Right website *The Right Stuff*. Richard Spencer has suggested that this is because, at least for some people, libertarianism is "a mask on white populism"[39]—a view shared by some on the left. As Conor Lynch noted in *Salon*, "While the libertarian movement as a whole is not inherently bigoted, and many believers despise intolerance, the ideology itself does attract many bigots who see the freedom-obsessed culture as a way to protect their 'right' of intolerance, and crack down on collective movements that fight for equality."[40] This may change as the more racist elements in libertarianism are drawn to the Alt-Right instead.

EUROPEAN RIGHT-WING MOVEMENTS

The general ideological thrust of the Alt-Right is completely disconnected from the American conservatism we have known since the 1950s. It has little interest in Edmund Burke or the American Founding Fathers. Its ideological moorings do not include any part of conservatism's core tenets—moral traditionalism, economic liberty, and a strong national defense. Its views on William F. Buckley and Ronald Reagan range from indifference to contempt. In many ways, the Alt-Right seems like a poor fit for the United States, where both the left and the right have roots in classical liberalism and the Enlightenment.

However, looking abroad, we can find examples of right-wing thought that mirror the Alt-Right. Europe is home to an older, more aristocratic, and less rational right-wing tradition, one that has rejected modern thinking from the beginning.[41] Different elements of the Alt-Right draw from different aspects of the European right. The most flamboyant and radical currents of the Alt-Right explicitly take their inspiration from the Third Reich. The neo-Nazi element of the Alt-Right, which is not insignificant, thinks Hitler's model for government was generally correct: the primary problem with Nazi Germany was that it lost the war.

The more intellectually sophisticated elements of the Alt-Right—such as those found at venues like *Counter-Currents*—tend to downplay the Nazi connection in favor of other right-wing European movements. The so-called European New Right (ENR) has been particularly influential on the Alt-Right, especially in its early days. The ENR was primarily a French movement begun by Alain de Benoist in the late 1960s and grounded in multiple ideological traditions. Although the ENR never endorsed the most violent and repressive right-wing regimes of the twentieth century, it leaned heavily on works from Weimar-era Germany, especially the "conservative revolutionaries" of that period: writers such as Ernst Jünger, Carl Schmitt, Oswald Spengler, and Arthur Moeller van den Bruck. These were thinkers that rejected both the communism of the Soviet Union and the liberalism of the United States, seeking to create a new form of government that preserved elements of traditionalism but was capable of standing up to the East and the West. Although all of these thinkers proposed ideas that were incorporated to some degree into Hitler's government, they did not all become proud Nazis—some opposed Hitler, some were ambivalent, and some were enthusiastic about the new government.

The European New Right resurrected many of these older ideas but also added new ideas typically associated with the left, favoring strong environmental protections and opposing colonialism. Some of its ideas on economics and the environment came from the political left, but its opposition to immigration and multiculturalism make it a distinctly right-wing movement. The ENR was particularly unique in that, in contrast to most French conservatives since the revolution of 1789, it had no interest in traditional Catholicism. Benoist is a staunch anti-Christian, viewing Christianity as one of the major explanations for the West's decline.

The ENR influenced a number of highbrow white nationalists—Benoist, for example, has spoken at the American Renaissance conference. ENR ideas were also frequently discussed among the Alt-Right during its first incarnation. This connection seems weaker now, however. Few among the new crop of online right-wing trolls and activists cite Benoist's *On Being a Pagan*.[42]

For most of its history, the ENR was not interested in mainstream politics or grassroots activism. Benoist and others were instead looking to build a philosophical foundation for a postliberal order, preferring "metapolitics" to practical politics. This is changing, however, as the European far right has begun to make its presence known outside of obscure journals. In the early 2000s, the so-called identitarian movement emerged in France, subsequently spreading to other European countries.[43] This movement has engaged in high-profile activism, including the occupation of mosques, and has been bolstered by the recent refugee crisis spurred by the conflict in Syria. Identitarians tend to be young and disconnected from traditional conservatism, and they have been emboldened by a new breed of populist, right-wing politicians. In this they are similar to Alt-Right supporters. Far-right parties have recently made impressive gains across the continent, seeing growing support in countries including France, Austria, and Sweden.

THE ANTI-IMMIGRATION MOVEMENTS

Unlike the Alt-Right, which is unwaveringly hostile to mass immigration, conservatives have never been unified on the immigration question. It is true that self-described conservatives in the electorate are much more likely to support immigration restrictions than self-described liberals. But adopting a conservative political philosophy does not necessarily lead one to favor border walls. In fact, many conservatives focused on economic concerns view immigration as a good thing. In 1984, the *Wall Street Journal* proposed the following constitutional amendment: "There shall be open borders."[44] Ronald Reagan famously signed legislation that offered a pathway to citizenship to undocumented immigrants. George W. Bush supported similar legislation during his presidency, as has John McCain throughout his Senate career.[45]

However, there are many mainstream conservatives that argue against large-scale immigration, especially undocumented immigration. In the political arena, recent efforts to pass liberalizing immigration reforms were blocked by conservative Republicans in the House of Representatives. And within the conservative media, we can find many voices calling for stronger immigration-enforcement efforts.

The conservative movement's high point of immigration restrictionism arguably occurred during the 1990s. This was the period when Buchanan shook up the GOP presidential primaries and where the high-immigration state of California passed several controversial ballot measures—Proposition 187, Proposition 209, and Proposition 227—which were presumably going to decrease both the amount of immigration to the state and minimize the effects of that immigration.

Although hostility toward high levels of immigration has always been a prominent feature of the more populist elements of conservative media—especially talk radio—restrictionist views have also been featured in many of the more highbrow journals of conservative opinion. *National Review*, for example, held a fairly strong stance against undocumented immigration during the 1990s. This was particularly true during the period when John O'Sullivan and Peter Brimelow were both editors at the magazine. Brimelow in particular was a vocal immigration opponent (though he is an immigrant) and is perhaps best known as the author of the anti-immigration book *Alien Nation*.[46]

National Review's stance on immigration seemed to soften somewhat when Rich Lowry took the helm, though it continued to editorialize against immigration-reform proposals that would have provided a pathway to citizenship for the undocumented.[47] Brimelow eventually left the magazine and began working on his own project, VDare.com, which was focused entirely on the immigration issue and much more explicitly racial than mainstream conservative publications and websites. This is why Brimelow is no longer welcome within the conservative movement's ranks. For his part, Brimelow denies that VDare is a white-nationalist webzine or even part of the Alt-Right—though he acknowledges that the label does fit some of VDare's contributors.[48]

Although the immigration issue animates the Alt-Right more than any other question of public policy (and on substance it agrees with much of what the anti-immigration voices in the mainstream have said on the subject), we should make a clear distinction. The mainstream conservative movement is generally careful never to discuss the immigration issue as being fundamentally about race. Most immigration-restrictionist groups focus heavily on economics, especially on the supposed downward pressure that mass immigration places on wages. They often argue that undocumented immigrants receive more in government services than they pay in taxes. These are empirical statements and can be disputed, but they are not directly connected to race.

Even those conservative restrictionists that focus on the cultural side of immigration tend to sidestep racial questions. They generally discuss questions of assimilation, especially language acquisition and crime associated with undocumented immigrants. These talking points come close to the racial aspect of immigration restrictionism, but those using this rhetoric can plausibly deny that their opposition to mass immigration (documented or otherwise) is rooted in racial animus or anxiety.

This highlights another surprising dissimilarity between the Alt-Right and the immigration restrictionists on the mainstream right. On balance, the Alt-Right is actually less hostile to Islam than many conservatives with access to mainstream venues. This does not mean that the Alt-Right has anything favorable to say about the immigration of Muslims into Western countries—the Alt-Right cheered in unison when Donald Trump suggested a ban on Muslim immigration, and members were similarly supportive when he tried to implement a ban on immigration from several predominantly Muslim countries at the start of his presidency. However, mainstream conservatives typically oppose Muslim immigrants precisely because they are Muslim. That is, they believe there are elements of Islam that make Muslims a bad fit for Western societies. This kind of rhetoric has been a persistent theme in conservative books, websites, and talk radio since September 11. Mark Steyn, for example, has been warning of the dangers of Islamic immigration for years, most notably in his book *America Alone.* Glenn Beck more recently published a book titled *It IS About Islam*. Other prominent anti-Muslim conservatives include Pamela Geller (the author of *Stop the Islamization of America*) and Robert Spencer (the author of *The Truth About Muhammad*).[49]

While these conservatives focus heavily on the issue of terrorism when expressing hostility toward Muslim immigration, they have also long attacked Islam from the left. That is, they argue Muslims should be restricted from Europe and the United States because Islam is incompatible with modern liberal values. These authors selectively quote the Koran in order to prove that Muslims cannot accept religious diversity, hate homosexuals, do not believe in democracy, and oppress women. Thus, until Islam is reformed and makes peace with the modern world, Muslims should not be welcomed into non-Muslim countries. According to Steyn, the West must "choose between liberty and mass Muslim immigration."[50]

The Alt-Right approaches the subject differently. Because it is so obsessed with race per se, it does not really care about the tenets of Islam. If all Muslims converted to Christianity (or abandoned religion entirely), most of the Alt-Right would be just as opposed to large-scale immigration from the Middle

East, South Asia, and the predominantly Muslim countries in Africa. So, perhaps ironically, people on the Alt-Right are less Islamophobic than many mainstream conservatives. But this is precisely because they are both more racist and because they do not care about the liberal values that Muslims ostensibly oppose.

THE MAINSTREAM CONSERVATIVE WAR ON POLITICAL CORRECTNESS

The genealogical link between mainstream conservatives and the Alt-Right, as I have emphasized, is weak. Unlike some commentators,[51] I do not see much of a connection between, say, the Tea Party and the Alt-Right. The Alt-Right views itself as entirely separate from mainstream conservatism—and to a great extent it is.

Yet there are parallels between the Alt-Right and certain elements of American conservatism, parallels that lend a certain irony to the conservative war on the Alt-Right. Conservatives have been quick to argue that the Alt-Right should be condemned as a racist movement. But in doing so, conservatives can sound like the so-called commissars of political correctness that they have mocked and condemned for years in articles and entire books.[52] This creates a problem for conservatives, who are in an awkward rhetorical position when faced with the Alt-Right.

Conservatives have long promoted their movement as being "politically incorrect." According to their own narrative, conservatives do not get upset about "microaggressions"; conservatives do not get worked up about off-color jokes; conservatives are tough and "tell it like it is"; conservatives are edgy. According to certain conservatives, those that complain about offensive speech are simply overprotected "snowflakes" who cannot take a joke. Some conservatives even argue that the "language police" are a threat to America. As Steve Tobak put it in a column for *Fox Business*: "While it's clear that political correctness is reflective of our societal norms, it also influences where our culture is heading. If I'm not mistaken, it's turning us into a nation of people who look like adults but act like entitled children, who act out when they don't get what they want or feel they deserve."[53] According to many conservative pundits, complaints from college students, academics, and the mainstream media about public displays of racism and intolerance are signs that America is becoming weak, that it is trading freedom of speech for "safe spaces." As many college campuses faced controversy and protest in 2015, conservative writers were quick to condemn protesters as "idiot children."[54]

This does not characterize all conservatives, of course. Many leading conservatives maintain a civil and respectful tone and use language that few could find objectionable. But the populist wing of the conservative movement has historically acted as though offensiveness is itself a virtue and that shocking liberal sensibilities is always a good thing. This leaves conservatives in a quandary. They want to distance themselves from the Alt-Right's rhetoric about historically disadvantaged populations. But in doing so, they invariably use language borrowed from the left, using terms like "racist," "nativist," and "misogynist." They do so after telling a generation of grassroots conservatives that anyone who uses those terms is a totalitarian.

As a result, the Alt-Right can effectively use the conservative movement's own rhetoric in response. Anti-Alt-Right conservatives such as Ben Shapiro, one of many conservatives to build a career on attacking political correctness,[55] are now targets of vitriol from the Alt-Right on the grounds that they are politically correct "social-justice warriors." This development has been noted by some on the left. As the headline of a piece by Robyn Pennachia noted in *Gawker*: "Ben Shapiro Declared a Social Justice Warrior by People More Racist Than Ben Shapiro."[56]

Conservatives are left without an obvious solution to this conundrum. They can stop condemning the Alt-Right for its outrageous comments; this risks conservatism being forever associated with the Alt-Right and its rhetoric. Alternatively, they can abandon the idea that conservatism is about rejecting political correctness and risk alienating those attracted to conservatism precisely because it is perceived as edgy and politically incorrect. Finally, conservatives can argue that they still oppose political correctness but that the Alt-Right crosses the line dividing politically incorrect speech from hate speech; this strategy may be the least risky, but it leaves conservatives in the precarious position of policing a line that is not clearly defined. Meanwhile, the Alt-Right will continue to insist that any critique of offensive speech amounts to capitulation.

To be clear: I do not think that conservatives who condemned political correctness represent a protoversion of the Alt-Right. Nonetheless, conservatives are at least somewhat responsible for the rise of the Alt-Right. Certain elements of the conservative movement have effectively delegitimized complaints about hate speech and racism. Some conservatives have concurred with this argument. As the conservative columnist Matt Lewis put it when I asked if conservatives bear any responsibility for the rise of the Alt-Right:

> We tolerated and even sometimes promoted conservative "entertainment" figures like Ann Coulter and outlets

like Breitbart.com who are now (to some degree, at least) promoting Alt-Right ideas. Meanwhile, the failure of GOP establishment elites to stop the leftward cultural drift also opens up room for the emergence of a radical, more muscular, movement on the Right.[57]

OTHER ONLINE MOVEMENTS

Before the Alt-Right entered the public consciousness, there were other predominantly online movements with obvious similarities. Two worth mentioning (which have been tied by some directly to the Alt-Right) are the Neo-Reaction movement and the Gamergate controversy. Although there are commonalities between these and the Alt-Right, they should be viewed as separate movements.

Like the Alt-Right, Neo-Reaction (often abbreviated NRx and also known as the Dark Enlightenment) is predominantly—maybe exclusively—online. It is also quite explicitly right wing in that it rejects egalitarianism, perhaps to a greater extent than the Alt-Right. NRx has none of the lowbrow qualities of the Alt-Right (it favors long essays over tweets and memes), and it exhibits a kind of high-IQ misanthropy. This is one reason it rejects democracy, which according to NRx gives undeserving people a say in a government that they do not, and cannot, understand, and argues instead for government that is monarchical or has some kind of corporate structure.[58]

Similar to the Alt-Right, NRx does not exhibit any of the American patriotism that is traditionally associated with the right. Some NRx writers even argue that the American Revolution represented the triumph of evil.[59] But unlike some figures on the Alt-Right, I am aware of no one associated with

NRx that ever harbored illusions of representing a current or future mass movement.

Some have suggested that NRx is an intellectual forebear of the Alt-Right.[60] This seems plausible, as there is some overlap in the arguments made by both camps. And many people read and identify with both. (It is still common to see comments on Twitter that include both an NRx hashtag and an Alt-Right hashtag.) But the Alt-Right did not grow out of NRx. To begin with, although most of the major figures associated with NRx (for example, Mencius Moldbug and the philosopher Nick Land) believe in nontrivial racial differences rooted in genetics, they do not support white nationalism. This is not because they believe racism is wrong but because white nationalism is *too democratic*. To quote Moldbug:

> And the worst thing about white nationalism, in my opinion, is just that it's nationalism. Nationalism is really another word for democracy—the concept of democracy makes no sense except as an algorithm for determining the General Will of the People, that is, the Nation. And whatever its electoral formula or lack thereof, every nationalist government has seen itself as in some sense a representative of the Volk.[61]

More importantly, while there was overlap in readership, and while some people did make their way from NRx to the Alt-Right,[62] NRx and the Alt-Right (at least in its first incarnation) developed independently of each other. I can find no evidence that the essayists involved with the original Alt-Right publications (*Taki's Magazine*, *Alternative Right*) seriously engaged with the ideas being put forth by the writers associated with NRx. A blogger that identifies with NRx similarly told me that "the two movements draw from largely different inspirations & thinkers of the past, with just a few exceptions."[63]

Regardless of how the two movements were once connected, the issue is now largely irrelevant. Interest in NRx appears to be waning. Moldbug stopped updating his blog in early 2016, stating that the site had "completed its mission."[64] Other webzines associated with NRx continue to operate, such as *Social Matter*, but at present the movement does not appear to be growing, and journalists covering the far right seem to have lost interest in it.

Gamergate, an online harassment campaign that occurred mostly in 2014, has also been seen as related to the Alt-Right. If NRx shared some of the philosophical premises of the Alt-Right but differed in strategy and tone, Gamergate shared the contemporary Alt-Right's style but little of its substance. To people with no connection to the world of video games, the details of Gamergate and the controversies surrounding it can be baffling.

Gamergate started as a controversy about ethics in video-game journalism—not the sort of thing that usually attracts national attention. A game designer named Zoe Quinn released a text-based video game called Depression Quest, and soon she was accused of trading sex for favorable reviews of the game.[65] Angry gamers left thousands of comments on Twitter and 4chan and began a sustained campaign against Quinn and other women who came to her defense. The end result was a victory for the online mob. Gamergate supporters successfully lobbied advertisers to withdraw from a number of publications. *Gawker*, for example, lost advertising revenue from corporations such as Mercedes-Benz as a result of these efforts.[66]

Gamergate showed that an army of anonymous activists and trolls can have a substantial and lasting impact on real-world organizations. It demonstrated that Internet mobs can be more than an annoyance. Gamergate had no leaders in the conventional sense, just loose coordination, largely through message boards. According to Max Read, former editor-in-chief of the now-defunct website *Gawker*: "Of all the enemies *Gawker* had made over the years—in New York media, in Silicon Valley, in Hollywood—none were more effective than the Gamergaters."[67] Read went on:

> Gamergate proved the power of well-organized reactionaries to threaten *Gawker*'s well-being. And when *Gawker* really went too far—far enough that even our regular defenders in the media wouldn't step up to speak for us—Gamergate was there, in the background, turning every crisis up a notch or two and making continued existence impossible.[68]

This method of persistent, coordinated trolling has since been embraced by the Alt-Right and helped it break into the mainstream discussion. But it does not imply that the same people were involved in both movements, although there is some overlap. Milo Yiannopoulos (who will be discussed in detail in subsequent chapters) wrote a great deal about Gamergate, but he is not really part of the Alt-Right. Gamergate mostly raised questions of misogyny, and while the Alt-Right is definitely antifeminist, race is their primary concern. Ian Miles Cheong wrote the following on the conservative webzine *Heat Street*: "it would be completely false to claim that GamerGate and the alt-right are the same thing."[69] Cheong also provided survey data indicating that Gamergate supporters actually tended to fall on the progressive end of the political spectrum.

One final online trend that more directly presaged the Alt-Right was Bob Whitaker's online campaign to promote the idea of "White Genocide." For years, Whitaker has been encouraging his followers to infiltrate the comment sections of major news stories and spread the mantra "anti-racist is a code word for anti-white."[70] Although Whitaker's name does not come up often in discussions about the Alt-Right, this was one of the first coordinated trolling campaigns conducted online by white nationalists. Matt Parrot, a longtime white-nationalist activist, suggested that Whitaker is the Alt-Right's "true godfather."[71]

CONCLUSION

The Alt-Right's precise genealogy is tricky to nail down. The basic premises of its worldview were clearly shared by earlier white-nationalist movements, but, aside from highbrow white-nationalist groups such as American Renaissance, there are few direct connections between these earlier organizations and the Alt-Right. Many of the Alt-Right's critiques of the conservative movement clearly echo those of the defunct paleoconservative movement, but the paleos (with some exceptions) were not typically interested in race per se. The same can be said of libertarianism; in fact, most libertarians are forceful in their rejection of racism. There is a stronger connection between the Alt-Right and the European far right, but the two differ when it comes to tone and strategy—though that may change if we see new coordination between far-right movements on opposite sides of the Atlantic. And while conservatism and the Alt-Right have few shared premises, the conservative movement may have inadvertently opened a door for the Alt-Right with its ferocious opposition to all things related to political correctness and its skepticism about mass immigration. Although the Alt-Right has borrowed elements from many other movements, it should be treated as a genuinely new phenomenon, born in 2008.

2

THE FIRST WAVE OF THE ALT-RIGHT

Richard Spencer coined the term "Alt-Right" but acknowledges that it was the paleoconservative scholar Paul Gottfried who inspired it. Before Spencer had started using the phrase, Gottfried hinted that a new right-wing movement was forming, one that would continue to battle the neoconservatives now that his own movement (paleoconservatism) was exhausted. When I spoke to him about this, Spencer said:

> I do take credit for coining Alternative Right and Alt-Right . . . I would give Paul credit for planting the idea in my mind. There was an article called "A Paleo Epitaph"[1] that I remember talking to him about over many days or weeks. We wanted to talk and be realistic about where the paleoconservative movement was and why it just didn't make sense any more. I'll read it to you real quick. This is from April 7th, 2008: "Even now an alternative is coming into existence as a counterforce to neoconservative dominance. It consists mostly of younger (thirty-something) writers and political activists; and although they are still glaringly under-funded, this rising

> generation is building bridges on the right." I think it might be true that that line stuck in my head, and that was . . . the proto version of Alt-Right.[2]

Although Gottfried perceived an alternative right forming back in 2008, he does not claim to be the creator of the Alt-Right,[3] nor does he claim to be part of the Alt-Right as it now exists. Although he has some ideological affinities with the Alt-Right, he has criticized its methods[4] and has distanced himself from Spencer.[5] When I asked Gottfried for his thoughts on the Alt-Right, he once again made it clear that he opposes white nationalism, even though he shares many of the Alt-Right's critiques of contemporary America:

> The white nationalists in particular are living on another planet, as far as I can determine. The multiculturalism and the PC that they and I loathe was created by white Westerners. Blacks and other non-whites have been peripheral to the victory of an ideology based on white male Western self-disparagement. White nationalism is no more a cure for this problem than recommending to cancer patients that they practice sky diving to get rid of their malignancy. Moreover, Western white people have generally not been "nationalistic" about race. They've been nationalists about being Frenchmen, Germans, Poles, Russians, etc. Even if all races practice discrimination against racial out-groups, Western identity has centered on other commonalities. The white nationalists are just imitating the black nationalists, who may have modeled an artificial racial identity that never existed in Africa. Finally although the Altright claim to

be "radical traditionalists," I'm unaware of any social tradition they want to maintain.[6]

Finally, although it is true that Gottfried perceived an alternative right forming back in 2008, what he saw at the time was very different from the Alt-Right we know today. Specifically, in "A Paleo Epitaph" he predicted that a rising right-wing movement would be closely aligned with Ron Paul's movement: "Judging by its direction, this youthful Right will be more libertarian than traditionalist."[7]

THE ORIGIN OF THE TERM

Spencer first emerged as a political writer in 2007. Before this he was on track for an academic career, earning an MA from the University of Chicago and enrolled in a Ph.D. program at Duke University. His first major article, in which his views on race could already be inferred, was published in the *American Conservative*. The article dealt with the Duke lacrosse rape scandal, which erupted when several members of the Duke lacrosse team were falsely accused of raping an African American woman. Spencer declared that the case "left serious people with a sense that something has gone terribly wrong with Duke's academic culture."[8]

He dropped out of Duke shortly thereafter and took a position at the *American Conservative*. However, Spencer never seemed conservative in the typical sense. He has never hidden his atheism, once taking part in a public debate on the question "Is Christianity for wimps?"—arguing that it is.[9] He has never, to my knowledge, declared an affinity for limited government for its own sake, though he has praised certain libertarians (especially Murray Rothbard and Hans-Hermann Hoppe) and spoken at libertarian events.[10]

Spencer was eventually fired from the *American Conservative*—a magazine that, despite publishing many controversial writers, such as Patrick Buchanan and Sam Francis, could never be described as white nationalist or even particularly radical. In 2008, he took a position as the managing editor of *Taki's Top Drawer*, later renamed *Taki's Magazine*, which was founded by Taki Theodoracopulos. It was there that the Alt-Right concept was eventually born. Theodoracopulos has long been a controversial right-wing author and columnist and a vocal critic of the mainstream conservative movement. He helped found the *American Conservative* in 2002. When he launched his own magazine in 2007, Theodoracopulos gave the following justification:

> I want to shake up the stodgy world of so-called "conservative" opinion. For the past ten years at least, the conservative movement has been dominated by a bunch of pudgy, pasty-faced kids in bow-ties and blue blazers who spent their youths playing Risk in gothic dormitories, while sipping port and smoking their father's stolen cigars. Thanks to the tragedy of September 11, and a compliant and dim-witted president, these kids got the chance to play Risk with real soldiers, with American soldiers. Patriotic men and women are dying over in Iraq for a war that was never in America's interests. And now these spitball gunners, these chicken hawks, want to attack Iran, which is no threat to the U.S. at all. One thing I can tell you for sure, there may well be some atheists in foxholes, but you'll never find a neocon. They prefer to

> send blue-collar kids out to die on their behalf, so they get to feel macho and make up for all the times they got wedgies in prep school. It shall be our considered task to take on the chicken-hawks of this world, and give them wedgies again.[11]

The first contributors to the magazine were mostly typical libertarians and paleoconservatives. Paul Gottfried, Tom Piatak, and Justin Raimondo were among its early contributing editors. In its early years, it was certainly "politically incorrect" but not particularly unusual compared to other right-wing publications. It did not initially have an explicitly racial agenda, but the site slowly began to change in tone after Spencer replaced F. J. Sarto as the managing editor in January 2008.[12]

Under Spencer's leadership, *Taki's Magazine* continued to publish mainstream paleoconservatives and libertarians, but it also began to offer space to more controversial figures, including Jared Taylor.[13] The decision to publish Taylor's work was criticized by other contributors, such as John Zmirak, who called white nationalists the "sad sorority of skin."[14] Spencer at the time responded that "*Takimag* is not a 'white nationalist' website."[15]

Although *Taki's Magazine* took a sharp turn to the right under Spencer's leadership, it continued to publish authors with a wide range of perspectives. And when the words "Alternative Right" first began to be used at that site, it was clearly a broad umbrella term, covering just about anyone on the right who opposed the neoconservative movement. Support for Ron Paul's 2008 presidential campaign appeared to be one common denominator for most of these writers. Libertarians, localists, foreign-policy noninterventionists, and white supremacists all found Paul palatable, and all could have been properly classified as part of the Alt-Right as the term was then understood. In 2016, Spencer explained his own reasons for supporting Ron Paul during his first presidential bid:

> Ron Paul was a kind of Trump candidate. Ron Paul did not get nearly the amount of average Republican support as Donald Trump has. But Ron Paul really energized people. He became the candidate of the internet. He really energized people who were otherwise cynical about elections, who were otherwise on the sidelines, disdainful or apathetic. I was certainly one of them. In 2008 my views weren't completely different from what they are today, but I've evolved as everyone does. But I had certainly the same cynicism about elections. I don't think elections are the way you change the world. You change the world through major cultural changes. . . . But Ron Paul really energized me, and he energized millions of others, because he was an anti-system candidate. And Ron Paul came in the context of the George W. Bush years, the flag pin years of the conservative movement . . . [Ron Paul] is a genuinely radical figure that is actually a little bit incompatible with the American system, certainly with the banking system and the foreign policy establishment. Just the fact that he was doing this, that he was saying these things in a major debate was radical and was exciting and was energizing.[16]

In 2009, Spencer left *Taki's Magazine* to form a new venture, a website simply titled *Alternative Right.* Spencer explained this evolution to me as follows:

> I stopped working at *Taki's Magazine* around New Year's of 2009, and then on March 1st of 2010 I started *AlternativeRight.com*. In the meantime, in that two months, I did do some basic fundraising for *Alt-Right*, just to get it started. It was definitely a shoestring operation. At that point, if you look at the initial articles for *AlternativeRight.com*, that was the first stage of the Alt-Right really coming into its own. We actually published Kevin MacDonald . . . we published an article on "Why I'm a Pagan" by Stephen McNallen, we published Jared Taylor. It was immediately, something right out the gate, something very new. Similar to *American Renaissance*, it took race very seriously, but the difference of course was that it was a cultural webzine. I don't think there was anything really like it. It certainly drew on some currents that were already taking place, but it was a new thing. It certainly could remind you of some things with *VDare*, it could remind you of some things at [*American Renaissance*], it could remind you of some things at the *American Conservative*, it could remind you of some things at *LewRockwell.com*, or something like that. But the way it was put together was quite original.[17]

To my knowledge, there is no public list of the people who provided funds for *Alternative Right* and similar ventures—although it does appear that the VDare Foundation contributed some of the initial funding.[18] But despite being a "shoestring operation," *Alternative Right* was getting money from somewhere—the professionalism of the site set it apart from the many white-nationalist websites hosted at places such as WordPress and Blogspot. From the beginning, whoever was backing the project surely understood that it was to be more than just another "edgy" conservative or libertarian project. According to Greg Johnson of *Counter-Currents*, "the principal funders . . . regarded *Alternative Right* as a vehicle for White Nationalist entryism, and they would have blown it up rather than see it become anything else."[19]

Unlike conservatism and libertarianism, white nationalism and other radical right-wing movements do not have a deep pool of wealthy benefactors that can be depended upon to keep the movement afloat. Nor do white-nationalist organizations have impressive direct-mail operations that effectively raise massive sums of money for their cause. There is, however, at least one notorious and deep-pocketed philanthropist willing to back the racial right: William Regnery II.

Readers with even a passing familiarity with the conservative movement will recognize the name Regnery. The Regnery family has long played a pivotal role in the conservative movement through its publishing ventures. Henry Regnery provided the initial funding for the conservative newspaper *Human Events* in 1944. More significantly, Regnery Publishing helped launch the conservative movement when it published William F. Buckley's first book, *God and Man at Yale*, in 1951, and Russell Kirk's classic work *The Conservative Mind* in 1953. Since then, Regnery has been the leading publisher of conservative books.

Of the Regnery family today, William Regnery seems to be the black sheep, and he generally avoids the public spotlight. Whereas Regnery Publishing releases mainstream conservative material—as it always has—William's political position is much farther to the right, and he has long used his share of the family fortune to fund white-nationalist projects.

In 2001, Regnery founded the Charles Martel Society as a non-profit organization.[20] This is the organization that launched the *Occidental Quarterly*. In 2005, Regnery founded the National Policy Institute (NPI). Despite the innocuous name, NPI has since its inception been a white-nationalist organization. The organization was rather obscure and marginalized until Spencer was chosen as its new president in 2011, at which point *Alternative Right* became an NPI initiative.

Despite being a far-right website from the very beginning, *Alternative Right* differed from other white-nationalist websites (such as *American Renaissance* or the *Occidental Quarterly*) in that it was not single-mindedly focused on race. It included many articles on foreign policy, domestic politics, economics, and gender relations (always from an antifeminist perspective). There was also a period when more mainstream writers and academics were willing to provide content to *Alternative Right*. Early guests on the *Alternative Right* podcast included the libertarian historians David Gordon and Thomas Woods and the conservative historian E. Christian Kopff, who also contributed an article to the site.[21] None of the content provided by those figures was racist in any way.

Alternative Right did not immediately gain much attention from mainstream sources, though it was quickly denounced by the Southern Poverty Law Center.[22] It was also noticed and condemned by Tim Mak, a columnist at David Frum's website. Frum is a well-known figure in the conservative movement. Mak noted the irony of the alternative right's claim to be the enemy of political correctness while simultaneously trying to hide its radical right-wing views behind ambiguous and innocuous sounding terms. After interviewing Spencer, Mak noted the following:

> Instead of spouting racism, Alternative Right is engaging in the much more respectable-sounding analysis of "human biological diversity" and "socio-biology."
>
> Rather than railing against the beast that is first-wave feminism, Richard Spencer's magazine is actually writing about "paleo-masculinity."
>
> He's not reactionary—he's a "radical traditionalist"; He's not castigating race X's culture—he's being "literary."
>
> What makes this all the more ironic is that, despite his critique of the right, Spencer was strikingly skittish when I asked if his goal was to make conservatism more "racially conscious." "Racially conscious? That's a little bit of a 'hot word,'" said Spencer.[23]

It was not long before any skittishness on Spencer's part disappeared. *Alternative Right* quickly became a hub for openly racist material, though it did avoid the crude language associated with other hubs of online white nationalism such as Stormfront. It differed from other manifestations of the racist right in other ways, as well.

Alternative Right, from the very beginning, pushed a political philosophy completely disconnected from the American tradition. Many, though not all,[24] of the earlier white-nationalist writers and groups tended to drape themselves in the American flag, and many of them spoke the language of middle-class American conservatism. The KKK presented itself as a Christian organization defending traditional American Protestantism. If we disregard his views on race, George Lincoln Rockwell held mostly conventional conservative positions. The same could be said of David Duke during his political career in the late 1980s and early 1990s. Southern nationalists continued to admire America's Founding Fathers, believing the American project was working until Abraham Lincoln threatened "states' rights." *Alternative Right*, from the start, ignored the traditional symbols of the United States. It had no interest in mainstream conservative political theory and did not share conservatism's passion for free-market economics. This put *Alternative Right* in a strange place, ideologically. It clearly stood outside the mainstream liberal-conservative dichotomy. According to Spencer:

> I did not make this explicit, but when I was thinking about that new standpoint, it was one that had a different philosophical basis than the kind of quaint Anglo-American conservatism outlined in, say, Russell Kirk's *The Conservative Mind*. I was thinking about something like the French New Right, something like the traditionalism of [Julius] Evola, something like Nietzsche, German idealism, Heidegger. I just wanted to go to all these places that conservatives resisted. It was kind of a joke between Paul Gottfried and I that conservatives considered all these people to be liberal. They were liberal fascists because they didn't believe in free markets and family values or something.[25]

The theme of identity politics for white people was an essential aspect of the Alt-Right as soon as *Alternative Right* was founded. And while Spencer has not, at least in recent years, shied away from the term "white nationalist," he helped introduced a new term into the lexicon on the American far right, though one that had been in use in Europe for some time. When asked his ideology, Spencer refers to himself as an identitarian. When I asked him define this term for me, he said the following:

I would say that an identitarian asks the question "Who am I?" or "Who are we?" before he asks any other question. And so, whereas other political ideologies might be based on an economic theory or might be based on a religion or might be based on a social theory, identitarianism is really based on an identity. And I think there are some interesting implications to that, as well. What is an identity? We have multiple identities. I'm a man. I'm thirty-eight years old. I grew up in Texas, was born in Massachusetts. Someone else might be from Vermont and they are into *Star Trek.* Someone might be a half-Mexican half-Vietnamese person who is also on the city council of his town. So we have all of these different layers of identity, and these have to do with localities, they have to do with history, they have to do certainly with genetics and race. They have to do with all sorts of things. You can say that there are some concentric circles of identity, but maybe they are not always exactly concentric. We can sometimes be pulled in different directions by our identity.

But I would say that race is the foundation of identity. You can't run away from that. Whether you want to identify with race, race identifies with you. You are part of something bigger than yourself. Race has a history to it. Identitarianism, the way I'm talking about it, it might kind of seem warm and fuzzy. It might be like, when you visited Ireland, did you resonate to the music? Did you feel at home there? Where are you really from? It doesn't exactly matter where you are right now. Where you are from does ultimately influence who you are. I think you need to ask those questions first, and then you can start asking economic questions, foreign policy, and

> so on. But again, I think race is the foundation of identity. You can't really think about identity without that.[26]

THE DECLINE OF THE CONCEPT

Alternative Right grew its audience in the years following its launch, but it did not become a movement. And after two years, Spencer was tired of both the website and the entire Alt-Right concept. He stopped personally working with the website in 2012. In his final article before stepping down, Spencer said, "Looking back over the past two years, I feel that I have accomplished most of the goals I set for myself in founding AltRight, which was never meant to become an institution."[27] In that same article, Spencer also stated, "Don't worry—AlternativeRight.com won't go anywhere. I'll keep it 'live' so long as the Internet still flickers." Spencer subsequently began to focus on his new ventures, which included running the preexisting National Policy Institute, Washington Summit Publishers (a book-publishing company that publishes books from a white-nationalist perspective), and a new website and print journal, *Radix*.

From that point forward, *Alternative Right* was coedited by Collin Lidell and Andy Nowicki. Although Spencer no longer had direct editorial control over the site, he remained its owner. And because *Alternative Right* was still generally known (among those who knew about it at all) as "Richard Spencer's website," he was automatically associated with new controversial material that appeared there—to his apparent frustration. Spencer was particularly concerned about some of Liddell's "outlandish and offensive" content (including an article with the title "Is Black Genocide Right?"), which was then used to attack Spencer in mainstream-media venues, despite the fact that the material appeared after he had relinquished editorial control of the site.[28]

In December 2013, Spencer shut down *Alternative Right*, apparently without first notifying its new editors. This decision created some controversy on the far right, and Lidell began complaining bitterly about this on other sites. In a Facebook post, the editors of *Radix* responded to the controversy by saying, "From the onset, the *Alternative Right* was conceived as a bold experiment and a short-term project to differentiate itself from the American conservative movement. It was never meant to be a long-term institution and, indeed, never was."[29]

In a podcast in which he explained the logic of leaving *Alternative Right* and creating *Radix*, Spencer stated:

> *Alternative Right*, calling it that did kind of wear on me. It never struck me as satisfying at all. Because, as you say, it really is kind of a negative conception of who we are. You're alternative to what? And putting even the "right" in there kind of limits us to, you know, the left-right division that was created after the French Revolution. I really thought that there has to be something more. If I were to describe myself, I would say that I still am motivated by the same German idealism that I had been motivated by for a long time. I think race is a very important part of that. I would say I am a white nationalist, but not one who simply wants to defend whites as they are, or defend whites in themselves. You know, as if I would be happy if some white person were elected. Like, "Oh, look, one of our own is in office! That's great. Yippee!" I want something very different. I want us, our whole civilization, to become itself. So I would say a tra-

> ditionalist futurist, archeo-futurist, motivated by German idealism and nationalism, that's pretty much who I am. I want our civilization to kind of rediscover itself, rediscover a lot of its Faustian qualities, its desire for exploration, for risk taking, for shooting for the stars, to put it banally.[30]

Within that same podcast, Spencer again reiterated that he wanted to "move beyond the alternative-right concept." Over five years, the alternative-right concept had shifted from a general description of anyone on the right who rejected the conservative movement to a term that was explicitly associated with white identity politics. But when the term was rejected by the person who coined it, it looked as though as though the alternative right was dead as a concept. Spencer's ambivalence about the term was shared by Jared Taylor, who told me:

> I have never liked the term Alt Right. Needless to say, I think my views on race differences (and sex differences if we are to include them in the Alt Right) are not an "alternate" view, in the casual way that a Merlot may be an alternate to a Cabernet. They are true, and the egalitarian view is false. Truth is no more an "alternative" to falsehood than health is an "alternative" to sickness.
>
> Likewise, I don't think there is anything inherently "right" about these ideas, any more than a heliocentric universe is "right" and a geocentric universe was "left." Societies with scientific views of race and sex (if we ever emerge from this obscurantist nightmare) will have a "right" and a "left" just like all societies. One can fully understand race and still support the welfare state, marriage

> for homosexuals, abortion on demand, cuts in defense spending, etc. I don't want to chase away potential allies by adopting an unnecessarily confining label. But expressions become popular entirely on their own.[31]

After the original *Alternative Right* website was shut down, Liddell and Nowicki created a new website (also called *Alternative Right*), but it did not have the same reach as the original venture.[32] And Liddell and Nowicki were not in a strong position to be prominent figures in the American white-nationalist movement. Liddell lived in Japan, and Nowicki, who among other things has declared (with seeming sincerity) that he has no problem with interracial marriage,[33] is not a white nationalist himself.

CONCLUSION

Aside from the new Alternative Right website and a few message boards, the term Alt-Right seemed to have fallen out of favor among the racial right on the Internet by 2014. However, no new term ever really arose to take its place. As a new iteration of the radical right began to grow, it needed something to call itself, and "Alt-Right" was available. But as we will see in the next chapter, when the Alt-Right emerged a second time, it went in a very different direction.

3

THE ALT-RIGHT RETURNS

Following the demise of the original *Alternative Right* website, it appeared that the Alt-Right as a label (though obviously not white nationalism as an idea) was finished. Aside from the new *Alternative Right* website, the phrase "Alternative Right" appeared to live on only in a few dark corners of the Internet, namely, 4chan and Reddit. But in 2015, the term "Alt-Right" was suddenly and unexpectedly being used by the radical right at multiple venues, especially social media. But the new Alt-Right was different—though it was based on the same fundamental premises.

The original *Alternative Right*, although it discussed a large number of issues, could generally be counted as one of the few online sources for highbrow white-nationalist content. It generally tried to maintain an intellectually serious tone as it promoted a racist and antiegalitarian worldview. The site's section dedicated to human biodiversity (HBD) contained endless discussions about the heritability of IQ—this was especially true of the articles contributed by Richard Hoste. It avoided racial slurs and the angry, hateful rhetoric of earlier white nationalists, instead favoring a tone reminiscent of the writings on race and eugenics written by early-twentieth-century progressives. The anti-Semitism at sites like *Alternative Right* maintained the academic jargon of people like Kevin MacDonald rather than the crude caricatures embraced by neo-Nazis.

This new alternative right, best known by the Twitter hashtag #AltRight, had none of the intellectual cover of its highbrow predecessor. It was ostentatiously vulgar and offensive, violating every contemporary taboo related to race, ethnicity, religion, and gender. Whereas the venues for highbrow white nationalism sought, with varying degrees of success, to present themselves as reasonable and serious, some elements of the new Alt-Right proudly flew the swastika and repeated the slogans of the older white-nationalist movement, such as "1488"—a number that combines the white nationalist David Lane's "Fourteen Words" ("We must secure the existence of our people and a future for white children") and a code for "Heil Hitler" (H is the eighth letter of the alphabet).[1] While some voices of the Alt-Right displayed these symbols and slogans earnestly, others, perhaps most, of the Alt-Right presented them in a peculiar way. The new Alt-Right put swastikas in Pepe's eyes because it was hilarious.

Although Spencer clearly takes pride in naming the Alt-Right and getting it off the ground, he also acknowledges that he was not responsible for its sudden resurgence:

> The Alt-Right is what it is today not because of me; it is what it is today because I let it go. I didn't possess it, and it was taken up by all these people. And so at this point, the Alt-Right is gigantic. It's even being used in Europe. . . . Alt-Right is the banner of resistance. It's the banner of European white identity politics. And it's also just the banner of general edginess.[2]

It does not appear that any one person can be credited for the resurgence of the Alt-Right as a popular term. From what I can tell, there was no strategy or plan behind it. Rather, in the years after Spencer shuttered the first *Alternative Right*, there was a growing white-identity movement online that did not really care for the term "white nationalist." It seems that people simply gravitated to the term Alt-Right because most people with those views were already aware of it and there was no obviously superior label. I asked the prolific Alt-Right blogger Lawrence Murray about this, and he largely concurred, telling me:

> I can only speak to my own experience on that but if I had to pin it down I would say the Republican primaries really galvanized the need to adopt a label that signaled the movement was opposed to both the mainline left and right, but intellectually proximate to the latter. Alternative right or Alt-Right was already floating around the circles I was most familiar with (*The Right Stuff*, *Counter-Currents*, and *Radix*).[3]

So "Alt-Right" became a catch-all term for this new racial right largely by default. A well-known Alt-Right podcaster who went by the name Jazzhands McFeels told me that the sudden growth of the movement pushed the acceptance of the label, in spite of some ambivalence about the term:

> When I came into the movement in late 2014, the term "Alt-Right" was sort of a forced meme that had been loosely applied by some prominent members of the movement. It was sort of a personal choice whether or not to use it. . . . As the movement began to coalesce,

> predominantly and almost exclusively online, the Alt-Right was used more frequently as a banner under which to rally. Once the media began referring to the movement as the Alt-Right, that was it.[4]

In its first iteration, Spencer was undoubtedly the leader of the Alt-Right, given that the term was associated with his websites. But now, although journalists understandably seek out, again and again, a small number of prominent figures on the Alt-Right when writing stories about the movement, the truth is that the Alt-Right is without leaders in the usual sense. It is a disorganized mob that broadly shares a number of goals and beliefs. Pepe did not become the unofficial mascot of the Alt-Right because there was a central figure telling his supporters to make Pepe their Twitter avatars but because someone decided Pepe was funny and others eventually agreed. As expressed by the neo-Nazi blogger Andrew Anglin:

> The movement is, at this point, entirely leaderless. The people involved in contributing to and/or consuming the content are on different Alt-Right sites and forums, many are on Twitter, reddit, 4chan, etc.
>
> There are minor "leaders," people who others listen to, but because there is yet to be an officially codified doctrine, no actual leader exists. The mob is the movement.[5]

WHITE NATIONALISM WITH A SMIRK

The new Alt-Right movement on the Internet differs in tone not just from *Alternative Right* and similar websites but also from the older white-nationalist movements. While it shares many of the same terms associated with skinheads and white-supremacist organizations like the KKK and National Alliance, its use of irony and humor clearly sets it apart. The movement does not display the kind of ostentatious bloodlust you see in older white-nationalist books like *The Turner Diaries*. Instead it has podcasts like *The Daily Shoah*, which has a banner copied from the Comedy Central series *The Daily Show*. Rosie Gray, then a journalist at *Buzzfeed*, noted this in an early article about the Alt-Right:

> The movement probably doesn't look like anything you've seen before. The alt right is loosely connected, and mostly online. The white nationalists of the alt right share more in common with European far-right movements than American ones. This is a movement that draws upon relatively obscure political theories like neoreaction or the "Dark Enlightenment," which reject the premises on which modernity is built, like democracy and egalitarianism. But it's not all so high-minded as that. Take a glance at the #altright hashtag on Twitter or at *The Right Stuff*, an online hub of the movement, and you'll find a penchant for aggressive rhetoric and outright racial and anti-Semitic slurs, often delivered in the arch, ironic tones common to modern internet discourse.[6]

Although Spencer and his webzines were clearly responsible for the creation of the Alt-Right as a concept, in terms of lingo and style, *Alternative Right* was probably not the most influential website in terms of shaping the Alt-Right as it exists today. As Gray suggests above, that title belongs to *The Right Stuff*, a site that publishes blog posts and podcasts from a large number of contributors. *TRS* first went online in 2012. Like the main venues for highbrow white nationalism (*Counter-Currents*, *American Renaissance*, the *Occidental Observer*, etc.), *TRS* posts lots of lengthy articles from a white-nationalist perspective. However, *TRS* has long been more open and in-your-face when it comes to racism. It did not shy away from racial slurs, for example, and even worked to popularize new ones, such as the phrase "Dindu Nuffins" as a term for African Americans. Many of the bizarre new terms associated with the Alt-Right appear to have been invented (or at least widely disseminated) at *TRS*.

And while the leading contributors to many highbrow white-nationalist websites wrote under their real names, most of the writers at *TRS* have used pennames. Most are unmistakably pennames, and some are absurdist: "Seventh Son," "Cocky Caucasian," "Alexandros Cuckington." The use of pseudonyms protects the identities of the writers—though, as I will discuss in the conclusion to this book, many of these writers have had their real identities exposed. But the use of pennames also limits the ability of many Alt-Right writers and podcasters to reach a wider audience easily. When journalists and academics are looking for someone on the Alt-Right to provide commentary, they typically turn to people willing to be completely open about both their views and their identities: people like Jared Taylor will probably always have a higher public profile than writers known only by names like "Bulbasaur."

The contemporary Alt-Right is a subset of the larger Internet troll culture, though Alt-Right trolls often have a serious purpose. For many years, well before anyone was using the term "Alt-Right," it was easy to find racial trolling in the comment sections of news stories, especially stories about race with an unmoderated comment section. Such comments often led to aggressive online disputes among readers. This is one reason many online news sources have begun aggressively moderating their comments, banning anonymous comments, or simply disabling comment sections.

TRS has taken the lead in promoting Alt-Right trolling. It has published multiple articles providing advice on how to be a more effective troll and explaining what trolling is supposed to accomplish. Although many trolls engage in these activities just for the fun of it, *TRS* takes the position that trolling is important:

> You should assume that you will never manage to convince your ideological enemies of the merit of your position. Rather, the purpose of trolling is to convince people reading your comments of the merit of your position. On many different web forums, lurkers outnumber posters by 10 to 1. The purpose of trolling raids is to convince these anonymous people, not the person you disagree with. As such, you can win hearts and minds even when met with universal opposition.[7]

TRS articles have also provided advice on how to troll as a team and have explained strategies for trolling different types of people and different kinds of Internet forums. Prompting large numbers of people simply to quit a particular venue is one of the more important victories a troll can achieve: "By dominating individual liberals and shifting the entire tone of the forum to the right, you can actually cause them to *Rage Quit* en masse. Of course once this happens, you'll need to change servers, but damn is it a beautiful thing to witness."[8]

The anonymous and trollish nature of the Alt-Right creates additional problems for outsiders who wish sincerely to understand the movement. Journalists and scholars that interview members of political movements need to be able to trust that they are receiving sincere answers. At the very least, when the person being interviewed masks his or her true views, we would expect them to do so for a practical reason, such as a desire to maintain social desirability. Problems arise when the person being interviewed lies simply because it is funny to do so.

One of the most high-profile cases of an anonymous Alt-Right supporter deceiving a journalist occurred when Olivia Nuzzi of the *Daily Beast* wrote a story on the origin of Pepe. She reached out to two prominent Alt-Right personae on Twitter: Paul Town and someone who went by the name "Jared Taylor Swift"—a combination of Jared Taylor and the singer Taylor Swift (a pop-culture figure who has been appropriated by the Alt-Right).[9] Swift gave Nuzzi a passionate defense of Pepe as a great symbol of the Alt-Right and suggested that there was a coordinated campaign to "reclaim Pepe from normies." In Alt-Right circles, a "normie" is a white person who is not part of the Alt-Right. Swift stated that Pepe is "a reflection of our souls, to most of us. It's disgusting to see people ('normies,' if you will) use him so trivially. He belongs to us. And we'll make him toxic if we have to."

The problem with this article was that both Swift and Town were apparently spouting total nonsense. A subsequent story published in the *Daily Caller* reported that there never was any kind of coordinated effort to control the use of Pepe.[10] In that story, Swift, who claimed still to be in high school, declared, "Basically, I interspersed various nuggets of truth and exaggerated a lot of things, and sometimes outright lied—in the interest of making a journalist believe that online Trump supporters are largely a group of meme-jihadis who use a cartoon frog to push Nazi propaganda. Because this was funny to me." Of course, we also cannot be confident that the *Daily Caller*'s follow-up story was entirely truthful, either. The Alt-Right's willingness to lie shamelessly only adds to the befuddlement of outsiders.

The Alt-Right pulled off an even more successful prank just days before the 2016 general election. On November 2, *Politico* ran a story about an Alt-Right plot to suppress minority turnout across the country.[11] Given the high level of racial polarization and social tension surrounding the election, concerns about violence at the polls were warranted. However, the claims made by the people quoted in the story were obviously implausible, if not ridiculous. For example, Mike Enoch, *TRS*'s owner, told the reporter:

> Many polling locations are in schools, and black schools are so disorderly that pretty much any official-looking white person with a clipboard can gain access to them ahead of time and set up a hidden camera. You don't really ever even have to speak with an adult. Simply walk in like you belong there and no one even asks you why you are there. So we usually go in teams of two, one person driving and one person dressed as a blue collar worker with a clipboard, and we set up a hidden camera in the school cafeteria. Go during lunchtime and the teachers are all so busy trying to contain the kids that no one says anything. We already have a few set up.

Enoch also said, "We also have some teams going in to the ghettos in Philly with 40s and weed to give out to the local residents which we think will lead to more of them staying home."

Neither claim was true. Subsequent stories in other venues revealed the prank. As Enoch told the *Daily Caller* the very next day: "This email . . . just rolled in, and I just saw it and thought I might play it a joke, and I never in a million years thought he'd print it. I was pretty sure he knew it was bullshit, but was then just going along with it for the fun of it, but it wasn't until the sixth response that he sent that I realized he was going to go ahead and print this crap."[12]

Although it is obvious that the writers and podcasters at *TRS* and similar venues are completely sincere in their racism and anti-Semitism, there is also a tongue-in-cheek element to their use of racial slurs and even a willingness to poke fun at the earnest radicalism of the earlier white nationalists. For example, Murdoch Murdoch, a group that creates satirical Alt-Right YouTube videos, has made videos mocking the unhinged genocidal lunacy of William Pierce.[13] As Jazzhands McFeels told me when I asked him about the role of humor in the Alt-Right: "Humor is one of the more effective tools we have at our disposal. Properly executed, it can be utilized to disarm our opposition, unravel their narratives, and pierce their arguments with elements of taboo truths we use to tactically nuke their agenda."[14]

A YOUNG MOVEMENT

People eager to enter a new era of racial egalitarianism have long had a great hope: that each generation is supposedly more progressive than the one that preceded it.[15] Yes, the Archie Bunker personalities are still out there, but they are getting older every year and will eventually be replaced entirely. The appearance of a new and youthful racist movement suggests these hopes have been overstated.

Estimating the demographic attributes of the Alt-Right requires a lot of guesswork. As it is anonymous and decentralized, it is not possible to determine how many people consider themselves part of the Alt-Right. That said, it is clear that the Alt-Right is much younger, on average, than previous iterations of the racial right in America. One can infer this youthfulness from the tone of the Alt-Right's Internet dialogue, but there is other evidence as well. Recent white-nationalist conferences—such as the conferences sponsored by the National Policy Institute—have had a large number of attendees under the age of thirty-five.

The relatively low median age at Alt-Right events is clearly a point of pride for their organizers, and one might be justly suspicious about these numbers. However, journalists who attended these events have independently confirmed that young people are a major presence. Writing about a 2013 NPI conference, Lauren Fox wrote in *Salon*: "Perhaps the most surprising thing about the conference were the number of young men present, millennials in search of a political identity."[16] The Southern Poverty Law Center similarly noted the large number of millennials at a recent NPI gathering.[17]

When I asked Spencer to describe the average supporter of the Alt-Right, he said the following:

> They are definitely predominantly secular, although that doesn't mean that you won't have someone who is a traditionalist in the Alt-Right. You will occasionally have traditionalist Protestants, Catholics; orthodoxy is a kind of fad. . . . I would say that it is no coincidence

> that so many in the Alt-Right are tech savvy or actually tech professionals . . . a lot of these people came to these ideas by reading not just news on the Internet but philosophy on the Internet and real analysis on the Internet. They were willing to go there. They were willing to get their philosophy from unusual sources, nonauthoritative sources in the sense of books that are given the imprimatur of a university press or something like that. If I were to sum up your average Alt-Righter, if we were to make a composite image of the Alt-Right, I would probably say someone who is thirty years old, who is a tech professional, who is an atheist, and who lives on one of the coasts.[18]

The question is why young people, including well-educated young people, are attracted to a movement like the Alt-Right at this time. In the past, the stereotypical young white nationalist was an angry, bitter skinhead with limited skills and prospects. So why would millennials who clearly have marketable skills be drawn into the Alt-Right? Until we can get some decent survey data from Alt-Right supporters, which may never happen, we can only speculate on this question. One common theme among the young Alt-Right supporters I interviewed was that growing racial polarization during the Obama administration—especially the coverage of the Trayvon Martin and Michael Brown shootings and the subsequent birth of the Black Lives Matter movement—pushed them to the right.

Some people within the Alt-Right have offered thoughts on why white nationalism has begun appealing to a larger demographic. Greg Johnson suggested that the Alt-Right is drawing in a higher caliber of people than earlier iterations of American white nationalism because the career prospects of college-educated whites have declined. In the recent past, a college degree was viewed as a guaranteed ticket to a middle-class lifestyle. Once people are financially secure and working a decent job, they are less drawn to radicalism. A growing number of young whites are returning home to live with their parents, remaining unemployed or underemployed for a long time, and their resentment grows. They also have a lot of free time to spend on the Internet. According to Johnson:

> White Nationalists, of course, are always bemoaning the lack of young people in our movement, especially middle-class, college-educated young people—the people who were brought up on the idea that they were "tomorrow's leaders." We are also, of course, given to bemoaning the fact that our best people are systematically coopted by the system. Their careers, families, and mortgages discourage them from taking unpopular stands.
>
> Well, the system is no longer coopting an astonishing number of young, middle-class, college-educated white men and women. White dispossession has worked its way to their demographic group too. They are intelligent, educated, and ambitious. They are also unemployed, idle, angry, and searching for answers. For White Nationalists, they are a vast, increasingly receptive audience, for we are the only ones offering honest explanations of what is happening to them and realistic, long-term solutions.[19]

The comparative youthfulness of the Alt-Right can further complicate the effort to trace its intellectual roots. The original Alt-Right was fairly literary, and the writers associated with the term at the time had a basic grasp of political theory and history. This is still the case today for many of the most prominent Alt-Right voices. But the young members of the current Alt-Right seem to have relied primarily on Internet message boards, vulgar Alt-Right websites, and social media for their education on these subjects. I suspect Lawrence Murray was largely correct when he told me that "there's a slight generation gap on the Alt-Right. You have one wing of more Gen X people who came through right-libertarianism, anarcho-capitalism, and paleoconservatism, but younger Millennials and now even a slice of Gen Z people now are coming straight through /pol/ or directly to Alt-Right outlets without having passed through anything else."[20] According to Murray, many on the Alt-Right may not have even been aware of earlier far-right movements before they aligned with the Alt-Right, noting, "I myself had never heard of Pierce or Duke for example until becoming involved with the Alt-Right."[21]

The youthfulness of the Alt-Right also probably accounts for many of the ways it differs from earlier white nationalism and paleoconservatism. These older movements were generally nostalgic and backward looking. They remember when the United States was overwhelmingly white, when multiculturalism was an abstraction rather than a lived reality. Even in those places that were diverse at the time, such as the South, there was a clear social hierarchy that benefitted whites in the mid–twentieth century. Most millennials do not have any memory of living in a country with those kinds of demographics or of benefitting from overt, unapologetic, and institutionalized racism. Early white nationalists pined for the America they remember and thus seemed to have a residual patriotism. This new crop of white nationalists, having grown up in a much more diverse United States, has never known an America that approximates the white-nationalist vision and thus seem willing to reject America—openly desiring the collapse of the country or the creation of a new white-nationalist regime that has nothing in common with the constitutional government the nation has known since its inception.[22]

MEME MAGIC

The Alt-Right is obsessed with memes, which is not surprising, as memes are now a major element of the Internet. An Internet meme is simply an image, video, idea, hashtag, or slogan that spreads virally online. The most famous Internet memes tend to be innocuous, such as funny cat pictures. The word "meme" was popularized by Richard Dawkins in his book *The Selfish Gene*. According to Dawkins:

> Examples of memes are tunes, ideas, catch-phrases, clothes, fashions, ways of making pots or of building arches. Just as genes propagate themselves in the gene pool by leaping from body to body via sperm or eggs, so memes propagate themselves in the meme pool by leaping from brain to brain via a process which, in the broad sense, can be called imitation. If a scientist hears, or reads about, a good idea, he passes it on to his colleagues and students. He mentions it in articles and his lectures. If the idea catches on, it can be said to propagate itself. . . . When you plant a fertile meme in my mind you literally parasitize my brain, turning it into a vehicle for the meme's propagation in just the way a virus may parasitize the genetic mechanism of the host cell.[23]

Although Internet memes are typically seen as a source of frivolous amusement—and much of the Alt-Right treats them that way—there is also a logic to Alt-Right memes. A dedicated cohort of Alt-Right propagandists, relentlessly pushing the more popular memes, are able to introduce terms and concepts into popular discussion, even among people who do not use social media. And it turns out that some of the most successful Alt-Right memes were initially pushed by a small number of Internet trolls but were eventually spread across social media, especially Twitter, largely by people with no affiliation with the Alt-Right. A study conducted by the Southern Poverty Law Center found that a handful of influential Twitter users (such as Mike Cernovich, who might be properly labeled as part of the "Alt-Lite," which I will discuss in chapter 6) were responsible for spreading the rumor that Hillary Clinton was in poor health—a notion that was eventually embraced by many people with no connection to the Alt-Right.[24]

There are few ways to know ahead of time which memes will ultimately break out of message boards such as 4chan and Reddit and permeate into the broader culture. The more successful memes tend to be those that are not ostentatiously racist and that have at least some plausible connection to reality. For example, toward the end of the 2016 presidential campaign, the Alt-Right began pushing a series of fake Clinton ads on social media with the hashtag #draftourdaughters,[25] often used along with the preexisting Clinton hashtag #StrongerTogether. The phony ads were premised on the notion that Clinton wanted women to register for the draft—which is actually true—but also suggested Clinton was eager to start a war with Russia and wanted women to be on the front lines. One of these ads showed a pregnant woman along with the text, "I am one month until my due date. And two months until I can fight for her."

Another successful meme, started at *The Right Stuff*, was the placement of three parentheses around Jewish names—(((Albert Einstein))), for example. The purpose of the parentheses was to highlight the large number of Jewish Americans in the media and academia. An Alt-Right supporter even created a Google Chrome plug-in called the "Coincidence Detector." The plug-in automatically put parentheses around Jewish-sounding names on web pages and was downloaded by thousands of people. Google quickly removed the plug-in for violating its hate-speech policies.[26]

As an act of defiance, a number of Jewish journalists (as well as other non-Jewish journalists) began to put their own names in parentheses. This only amused the Alt-Right. The point of the campaign was draw attention to the overrepresentation of Jews in the media. When Jewish media personalities began to do this to themselves, the Alt-Right considered it an even greater victory.[27]

The "Red Pill" is another common Alt-Right meme. This is an idea borrowed from the 1999 science-fiction film *The Matrix*. In the film, the character Morpheus gave the protagonist, Neo, a chance to take the "red pill," which would show him the true nature of reality, hidden from everyone else. After taking the pill, Neo's life could never be the same again. According to the Alt-Right, most white Americans ("normies") live in a fantasy world, believing myths propagated by progressives. But a person who takes the red pill is suddenly aware of purported biological racial differences, problems associated with racial diversity, and various conspiracy theories about Jewish subversion. On Alt-Right blogs and message boards, discussions of how individuals were "redpilled" are common, as are discussions about how to give other people the red pill.[28] Much of the Alt-Right also seems to agree that taking the red pill leads to an irresistible urge to get involved in the movement. When I asked an Alt-Right essayist who writes under the name Henry Olson why he began creating right-wing content, he said the following: "I do not think I have the option to ignore the important events going on around me. When our entire culture is under attack, I need to do what I can to fight back and try to protect it, even when my contribution is very small. Otherwise, all of the time I've spent reading would be for nothing; I could have just as well spent that time gardening or working on my tan."[29]

Aside from Pepe, the Alt-Right has also adopted other irreverent mascots. The "Moon Man," based on an anthropomorphic crescent moon used by the restaurant chain McDonald's as a mascot in the 1980s, has also been appropriated by the movement.[30] Alt-Right supporters have posted videos on YouTube depicting Moon Man rapping via a text-to-speech synthesizer. The lyrics to these songs—which have titles like "Black Lives Don't Matter"—are filled with racist invective.

There is a certain irony to the Alt-Right's success online. Especially following the 2008 presidential campaign, when Barack Obama's campaign skillfully used the Internet to outmaneuver both Hillary Clinton and John McCain, it looked like the left had a near-monopoly on successful online activism.[31] At that time, it seemed libertarians were the only people on the right with any talent for the medium. While the Tea Party movement successfully used the Internet to organize and mobilize, its online efforts were heavily supplemented by massive financial support and infrastructure in the real world.

The Alt-Right's ability to use the Internet more successfully than anyone else in 2016 was a shock to many people. As Douglas Haddow noted in the *Guardian*:

> Back in 2010, the idea of using memes to political ends was still housed within a fairly slim leftist-activist corridor—it was a tool that seemed entirely of our own creation, and entirely under our control. We viewed memes as a vehicle through which activists could speak truth to power—they were molotov Jpegs to be thrown at corporate hegemony's bulletproof limousine.
>
> Never in our most ironic dreams did we think that the spirit of our tired, lager-fueled pisstakes would end up leading to a resurgence of white nationalism and make the prospect of a fascist America faintly realistic.[32]

The instantaneous ability for readers to interact with a story and with one another was expected to improve democratic deliberation. Two researchers studying racism in news comment sections noted:

> The rise of many-to-many communication networks initially offered great promise for a "new public sphere" of citizen journalists and, at long last, an overthrow of corporate agenda-setting in political news gathering, reporting, and framing. In this new public sphere, the people—rather than news media pundits or news corporations—would (re)shape democratic discourse through direct participation.[33]

The reality proved to be very different.

LOOSE COORDINATION

Alt-Right memes and strategies tend to thrive or fade away organically, based on what is effective, rather than because a particular leader promotes them from above. But while many Alt-Right supporters really are working completely independently from the others, in certain circumstances supporters of the Alt-Right do coordinate, even if they do not know one another's identities. An Alt-Right supporter, who wished only to be known as "Brad," explained to me how different kinds of Alt-Right online activities typically occur: "It's both [coordinated and uncoordinated]. Depends. There's a constant background of independent, uncoordinated trolling. But even these memes are posted, copied, and modified. However, circumstances arise when attacks become more coordinated."

As an example of Alt-Right cooperation, Brad noted that a group on Reddit worked together to sift through the Hillary Clinton e-mails released through WikiLeaks, searching for damning material. Beyond Reddit, a Clinton opponent set up a website in July 2016 that was dedicated specifically to this project (http://clintonfoundationinvestigation.com/). At this site, readers were able to share conveniently any information that might be damaging to Clinton and subsequently to push this material into the broader conversation. The site also contained a massive repository of anti-Clinton memes that could be easily shared on social media or printed out and left in public places.

Other documents posted online provided advice on how to push a particular narrative during the presidential campaign. One anonymous Alt-Right supporter posted an article on "Advanced Meme Warfare" at the site pastebin.com.[34] According to the author of the piece:

> Successful guerilla PR / Astroturfing campaigns can be broken down into 3 simple steps:
>
> Step 1: Research
>
> Step 2: Content Creation
>
> Step 3: Outreach.
>
> Considering that The witch's [Clinton's] side owns almost the entirety of the [mainstream media], we're going to be facing an upward battle. That said, meme magic is real and our collective effort has the power to produce some pretty incredible results. With that said, I will chop this up into sections focusing on All three of these aspects plus some additional info on maintaining online privacy/safety and keeping your identity obscure.[35]

The article went on to explain how to create memes using the fonts associated with the Clinton campaign, how to create dummy Twitter accounts that would attract a large number of "normie" followers, how to manipulate journalists into following fake leads, and how to do all of the above without risking the loss of anonymity (by setting up private proxy servers, for example).

These and related documents demonstrate how sophisticated the Alt-Right's online disinformation campaign had become by the end of 2016. But even when highly complex, the Alt-Right's online activities were not the result of any central planning. Memes spread virally, guided by the invisible hand of the Internet market. When a strategy was effective and popular, it was imitated by others.

Whereas research and the creation of memes is often a collective affair, honed and perfected over time, online harassment of individuals is typically spontaneous. According to Brad: "What trolling coordination exists seems more content than target driven. Collaboration is done for research and generating memes. Not saying, 'Hey let's all attack this guy on Twitter.' Now, that said pile-ons do occur. But that's endemic to Twitter. People can see friends trolling and join in for the lulz."

The claim that the online harassment of specific individuals occurs spontaneously rather than as the result of a preconceived plan seems to be correct—though the Alt-Right has compiled contact information for well-known journalists.[36] But there are some common characteristics among people who receive Alt-Right harassment online. They tend to be public figures, especially journalists. This makes sense from a strategic perspective, as famous people typically have a large number of social-media followers—far more than the average Alt-Right account. The Alt-Right can capture the attention of these followers if it successfully baits such a person into a public dispute. Jewish journalists, mainstream conservative journalists, and progressive celebrities that attack Donald Trump or the Alt-Right directly are especially likely to receive online abuse from the Alt-Right.

Yet for all the abuse that the Alt-Right heaps on mainstream public figures, the movement also recognizes that it has largely depended upon these opponents for its own expansion. Had prominent writers never discussed the Alt-Right at their own venues (even to denounce the movement), it would likely have experienced slower growth. August J. Rush, the editor of an Alt-Right/NRx website called *Dissident Right*, suggested to me that Alt-Right trolls had successfully manipulated journalists into giving the movement more attention than it warranted at the time:

> The Alt-Right went from a tiny, fringe thing found on Twitter & /pol/ to being a major component of the 2016

> election. That's truly impressive, and I think that's mostly due to the unique lives of journalists. Their entire lives are lived online on sites like Twitter, and so what they see and report on tends to come to life through their articles—at times, it is a self-fulfilling prophecy. Normal people don't live their existence online on places like Twitter, so most people had no idea we existed. We essentially created a false reality for them where they were drowned in responses by our Great Troll Army, to the point where journalists began to become afraid to write anti-White content out of fear of the online backlash. . . . The Alt-Right literally did not have a physical presence until recently; we practically memed ourselves into existence through hijacking the OODA [observe, orient, decide, and act] loop of journalists, getting them to write about this scary, secretive, mean online group, and drawing more and more eyes & converts when people began to tune in to see what our platforms were.[37]

Rush makes an important point, one worth reiterating. As recently as 2015, the Alt-Right was largely a Potemkin village. A trifling number of keyboard activists concentrated their fire on a small number of famous figures on social media, giving important opinion leaders the impression that there was a massive white-nationalist army taking over Twitter. By simply engaging with these trolls online, and in some cases writing articles warning America about this supposedly dangerous menace, the Alt-Right's opponents gave them visibility they would not have had otherwise. Although many (perhaps most) of the people who learned about the Alt-Right because of this new exposure were horrified to learn of its existence, others thought it sounded like a fun, worthwhile movement and decided to join.

CONCLUSION

The Alt-Right is a radical right-wing movement perfectly suited for the Internet age. It knows how to speak to disaffected young millennials. It can quickly respond to current events and a changing media environment and can spontaneously coordinate, even in the absence of formal leadership. As an anonymous army of online trolls, it is remarkable that it made itself known in an election year when there was no shortage of breaking news that needed to be covered, bringing the far-right into the national discussion to a degree unseen since the end of David Duke's political career.

But the Alt-Right, even after Trump's victory, remains a powerless and marginalized group, and the organized conservative movement remains the primary opponent of the egalitarian left. For this reason, the Alt-Right wants to help facilitate the demise of conservatism.

4

THE ALT-RIGHT ATTACK ON THE CONSERVATIVE MOVEMENT

When discussing the Alt-Right, much of the analysis by journalists focuses, as it should, on the movement's attacks on racial and religious minorities. The Alt-Right's insults and online harassment of marginalized communities should not be downplayed. However, the main target of the Alt-Right's wrath, at least for now, is arguably not African Americans, Latinos, or political progressives; it is mainstream conservatives.

Many of the Alt-Right's complaints about the mainstream conservative movement echo those made by earlier right-wing movements, especially the paleoconservatives. But a key difference is that the paleoconservatives were interested in reforming conservatism, perhaps returning it to the philosophical foundation that it rested upon before the neoconservatives pushed it in a more egalitarian, progressive direction. According to a common paleoconservative view, conservatism could once again be a valuable political movement if it experienced a major change in leadership. The Alt-Right is very different. It does not care at all about limited government per se. It does not even share conservatism's passion for the basic symbols of American patriotism. Although there is diversity of opinion on the Alt-Right, it generally argues for something entirely distinct from conservatism and views the existence and strength of the conservative movement as a challenge to overcome. A key problem with conservatism, from the Alt-Right's perspective, is that it shares too many premises with liberalism (both classical and contemporary).

THE ALT-RIGHT CASE AGAINST CONSERVATISM

The Alt-Right's supporters may not agree on which philosophical premises undergird the movement, but I have never encountered anyone on the Alt-Right who believes the works of conservatives such as Russell Kirk, Frank Meyer, or Milton Friedman should serve as a primary source of inspiration. It consistently argues for beginning from a completely different foundation. In fact, the Alt-Right is calling for something even more radical than the rejection of American conservatism. The Alt-Right also rejects many of the basic premises of classical liberalism and the Enlightenment. This has been pointed out by some of the Alt-Right's opponents.[1]

The Alt-Right critiques the conservative movement for failing to recognize that the United States is now fundamentally different from what it was in the 1950s, when conservatism first emerged as a serious political force. Although conservatism is presumably based on abstract principles and in theory can appeal to people of all genders, racial groups, and religions, the reality is that conservatism has always been most appealing to people with specific demographic characteristics: financially secure white people living in suburbs and rural areas. Key figures in the Republican Party (with which conservatism has long been intimately connected) clearly recognized this—if they had not, there would have never been the Republican "Southern Strategy."[2] However, as a result of remarkable demographic changes since 1965, the primary constituents of conservative politics have been shrinking as a percentage of the overall electorate.

There are some notable parallels between how the mainstream left and the Alt-Right view the issue of demographic change and the GOP. The left has long pointed out that conservatism, as defined by the mainstream conservative movement, is not a winning platform in twenty-first-century America.[3] For this reason, the Republican Party needs to abandon those elements of conservatism that have limited appeal in today's demographic environment—an environment that will only become more challenging for conservatism in the coming decades. Like progressives, the Alt-Right similarly argues that conservatism as we know it is becoming obsolete. But rather than move left, the Alt-Right wants the Republican Party to embrace the hard right and push transparent white-identity politics, with the ultimate goal of stopping and even reversing these demographic trends.

A key problem with the mainstream conservative movement, according to many Alt-Right supporters, is that it refuses to take identity politics seriously. Since Nixon, conservatives have won elected office by appealing to white anxieties, but once in power, the Alt-Right argues, these conservatives never actually fought for the policies that their white voters really wanted. Ellison Lodge made this argument in *Taki's Magazine* in 2009:

> The Southern Strategy succeeded in electing Republicans, but they didn't even bother trying to do anything about immigration or [racial] quotas. Richard Nixon

> won by appropriating the language of George Wallace, but went on to increase the Civil Rights department's budget by 800 percent, institute the Philadelphia Plan for quotas, and a host of other left-wing racial policies. Reagan signed the 1986 amnesty bill. Bush I won with the Willie Horton ad, but went on to extend quotas with the renewed Civil Rights Act. In addition to his constant push for amnesty, Bush II encouraged the Supreme Court to uphold racial preferences in the Gratz and Grutter cases.[4]

The general Alt-Right critique of conservatism can be summed up as follows: white people are the predominant constituents of conservative politics, but conservatives in power rarely promote white interests. In fact, many conservatives consider it a point of pride that they do not promote white interests. Over the course of the 2016 election, the Alt-Right created a term for this kind of conservative.

"CUCKSERVATISM"

"Cuckservative"—a combination of the words cuckold and conservative—has been one of the Alt-Right's most successful memes. A cuckold is a man with a wife who has been unfaithful; it more specifically refers to a man who (knowingly or unknowingly) helps raise offspring that are not genetically his own. Although it is unclear who first coined the term, the meaning of "cuckservative" was explained by the right-wing blogger Alfred W. Clark: "Very basically, the cuckservative is a white gentile conservative (or libertarian) who thinks he's promoting his own interests but really isn't. In fact, the cuckservative is an extreme universalist and seems often to suffer from ethnomasochism & pathological altruism. In short, a cuckservative is a white (non-Jewish) conservative who isn't racially aware."[5]

Racist invective on Twitter is certainly not new. But the hashtag "#cuckservative" stood out because of the astonishing number of times it was used online and the large amount of media attention it received. According to the *New York Times*, the word was used five thousand times on Twitter in just one day.[6] Writing in the *New Republic*, Jeet Heer attempted to discern why the new word saw such a meteoric rise in use: "The term cuckservative is popular because it pushes psycho-sexual hot buttons. Racism and sexism have always been connected, with one of the prime justifications for racial hierarchy being the supposed need to protect white women from black men and also, more implicitly, to keep black women sexually submissive to white men."[7]

In hindsight, it seems that mainstream conservatives would have been better off simply ignoring the new insult, dismissing it as yet another irrelevant vulgar slur from a marginalized, irrelevant corner of the Internet. But a significant number of conservatives did not ignore the attack and instead began expressing their outrage about "#cuckservative."

Matt Lewis wrote multiple articles on the subject, explaining that he was doing so to alert readers of the term's real meaning:

> The danger is that otherwise well-meaning grassroots conservatives might mistakenly think this term, which, at best, is meant to be emasculating, was merely an anodyne synonym for RINO ["Republican in name only"—a term conservatives use for Republicans that

> do not work to advance conservative causes]. Instead, it's a rallying cry for white supremacists and "neoreactionaries" who, for whatever reason, seem to back Trump.[8]

Erick Erickson—a conservative radio host and vocal opponent of the Alt-Right and Donald Trump—emphasized that the people who used the term were not conservatives:

> The people who use the term "cuckservative" are racists, not conservative, and not Christian. They may claim to be Christian, but I have a hard time thinking anyone who sees the world in terms of skin color, instead of souls to be saved, is really meaningfully a Christian. Considering they routinely attack evangelical Christians for adopting outside their race or, you know, providing comfort to the children of illegal aliens who've been dropped off at the American border bewildered and abused, they sure are not acting on the faith they claim.[9]

As is often the case when challenging Internet trolls, Lewis's and Erickson's attacks on those who used the "cuckservative" slur not only drew fire from the Alt-Right but brought it to the attention of large numbers of people who would probably have never heard of it (Erickson alone has more than 150,000 followers on Twitter). Both figures became immediate sources of mockery by the Alt-Right on social media and various websites. Jeb Bush was another common recipient of the slur, largely because of his comparatively progressive stance on immigration and his Mexican-American wife.

Lewis's and Erickson's sentiments were shared by mainstream conservatives, who rejected the cuckservative concept and denounced those who used it. While Rush Limbaugh used language that was reminiscent of cuckservative ("If Trump were your average, ordinary, cuckolded Republican, he would have apologized by now, and he would have begged for forgiveness, and he would have gone away"),[10] there is no evidence that he was familiar with the slur at the time. To my knowledge, Milo Yiannopoulos, a writer and editor at *Breitbart*, is the only conservative with access to mainstream venues who defended the term.[11] Yiannopoulos is himself a controversial figure, best known for his vitriolic attacks on feminism and, more recently, for his comments that seemed to glorify pederasty. I will discuss both him and *Breitbart* in greater detail in chapter 7.

Shortly after the term was popularized, a short e-book on the "cuckservative" slur was released. *Cuckservative: How "Conservatives" Betrayed America* was written and published in 2015 by Vox Day and John Red Eagle.[12] The book claimed that, contrary to the mainstream conservative position, the United States is not a "proposition nation," one based upon abstract principles such as liberty and equality. According to Day and Red Eagle, the United States was always meant to be a country for a particular people with a shared ancestry—this was made clear in the preamble to the Constitution, which explicitly stated that it intended to "secure the blessings of liberty to ourselves and our posterity." The book states:

> The key phrase is this: "to ourselves and our posterity." The blessings of liberty are not to be secured to all the nations of the world, to the tired and huddled masses, or to the wretched refuse of the teeming shores of other lands. They are to be secured to our children, and their

> children, and their children's children. To sacrifice their interests to the interests of children in other lands is to betray both past and future America. It is to permit an alien posterity, like the newly hatched cuckoo in another bird's nest, to eliminate our own, and in doing so, defeat the purpose of the Constitution. It is, like the cuckolded husband, to raise the children of another man instead of one's own sons and daughters.[13]

Day and Red Eagle went on to argue against many of the common conservative and liberal talking points about the United States—such as the generally accepted notion that the United States is a "nation of immigrants"—and challenged the idea that immigrants tend, in the long run, to assimilate to American norms. Unsurprisingly, most of the book was dedicated to the subjects of demographics and immigration, but it also argued against the principle of free trade—one of the few points of near-uniform agreement within the mainstream conservative movement.

The Alt-Right was delighted by the rapid spread of the "cuckservative" meme and the furious response it received from conservative media. A writer using the pen name "Clear Above" explained at *The Right Stuff* what the Alt-Right had learned from the controversy:

> First, mass movements are overrated and individuals matter. #Cuckservative was from the beginning astroturfed, pushed by a small number of highly dedicated individuals backed by a small number of article writers and meme creators. Popular movements are overvalued—we only need a few hundred people, at most, to affect the

> course of public policy. Our problem is one of coordination, not numbers.
>
> Second, #cuckservative revealed the ideal level of edginess. Obviously, opinions inside the Overton window are useless, while Ben Garrison levels of hatred will simply get us ignored and shunned. #Cuckservative evidently hit a sweet spot, presenting a message that was usually but not invariably racial in nature. This put us in a position where people would listen to our message instead of rejecting it out of hand. Going forward, we should strive for this level of edginess: probably racially aware, but with plausible deniability.[14]

Scholarly research confirmed that, within any online social movement, a small number of "buzzmakers" can have a disproportionate impact.[15] A quick glance at the hashtags associated with the Alt-Right demonstrates this is true—a relatively small number of accounts have created a large percentage of the overall number of tweets. Clear Above's second point is particularly important for understanding the strategy of the Alt-Right. Experience has taught the radical right that the older white-nationalist movement's preferred tactics—such as marching in Nazi uniforms or KKK robes—are less than worthless when it comes to spreading its message; normal people are turned off by such methods. On the other hand, if the Alt-Right were entirely to hide its racial agenda and attempt to blend in with mainstream conservatives, its effect would be negligible. Forcing a change in the conversation instead requires a balancing act between the two extremes. The Alt-Right, more than any radical right-wing movement in recent history, seems to have found that balance.

AGAINST THE RELIGIOUS RIGHT

The Alt-Right is (for the most part) secular in its orientation and hostile to the politicized Christianity that dominated Republican politics since the late 1970s. For a generation, the secular left viewed the religious right as the greatest obstacle to the creation of an open and tolerant society; it now appears that the postreligious may be more threatening to fundamental liberal values than the religious right ever was.

For many on the Alt-Right, the religious right represents most of what it opposes. Some of the Alt-Right is opposed to Christianity as such. Nietzsche is cited by Richard Spencer and others associated with the movement as an inspiration, which itself is a major departure from mainstream conservatives, who for years have railed against the nineteenth-century German philosopher and his influence. The conservative newspaper *Human Events* listed *Beyond Good and Evil* as one of the top ten most harmful books of the last two hundred years, along with *The Communist Manifesto, Mein Kampf,* and *Quotations from Chairman Mao.*[16]

Unlike most conservatives, much of the Alt-Right nods along with Nietzsche's critique of Christianity and its "slave morality" and views the Christian worldview as a hindrance to the rediscovery of aristocratic values. According to elements of the radical right, despite formally repudiating Christian conservatives and often rejecting religion entirely, liberals still maintain a basic Christian ethos: a sense of guilt, a belief in atonement, and the idea that weakness is a measure of moral superiority.[17]

The Alt-Right also critiques Christianity as a universal religion equally open to all people. This is rooted in the Gospels and seems an inescapable element of the faith ("There is neither Jew nor Greek, there is neither bond nor free, there is neither male nor female: for ye are all one in Christ Jesus").[18] This belief in a spiritual unity of all mankind presumably weakens the ability of particular ethnic and racial groups to favor their own people.

Christianity's Jewish roots are another source of far-right hostility toward the religion. Even among those white nationalists who are less hostile to Jews, there is a sense that Christianity is a foreign religion imposed on Europeans, and for that reason, Europeans should reject it. If they insist on having some kind of religious attachment, it should be an indigenous European faith—like the Norse or Greco-Roman religions.[19] But for the anti-Semitic element of the far right, Christianity is a major problem because of the central role that Jews play in Christian history and theology. According to the Alt-Right, the notion that Jews are "God's chosen people" provides Jews a special status in the minds of many Christians (never mind that for much of its history, Christianity exhibited great hostility toward Jews).[20]

Even greater than its criticism of the religion is the Alt-Right's criticism of politicized Christianity, which has long been a powerful force in the United States and which the Alt-Right views as a major hindrance to the development of explicit white-identity politics.

This may at first seem odd given that, in many ways, the religious right has been on the farthest right-wing fringes of the conservative movement. Jerry Falwell was no leftist, and it is clear that there was at least some racial angle to the rise of the religious right—fury at being forced to integrate schools appears to have one reason the religious right exploded onto the political scene in the 1970s.[21]

But the religious right has been undergoing a slow change. Most of the original major voices associated with the religious right are now deceased or well into their retirement, and the evangelical leaders that have replaced them are not particularly right wing. We now increasingly hear evangelicals speaking out on issues relating to social and economic justice and downplaying their traditional political issues such as abortion, gay marriage, and prayer in school.

Although the rank-and-file white evangelicals remain as Republican and conservative on many issues as ever (white evangelicals voted overwhelmingly for Trump), many of the people at the top of their religious institutions are not. Even the famously conservative Southern Baptist Convention has made significant moves to the political left on critical issues. For example, in 2011 the SBC called for immigration reform that would provide undocumented immigrants with "a just and compassionate path to legal status."[22] More recently, the SBC endorsed efforts to invite refugees from war-torn countries into the United States, resolving "That we encourage Southern Baptist churches and families to welcome and adopt refugees into their churches and homes as a means to demonstrate to the nations that our God longs for every tribe, tongue, and nation to be welcomed at His Throne."[23]

The SBC has also taken a new stance on the issue of the Confederate battle flag. Although supporters of the flag are surely overrepresented among SBC ranks, the denomination nonetheless resolved in 2016 "That we call our brothers and sisters in Christ to discontinue the display of the Confederate battle flag as a sign of solidarity of the whole Body of Christ, including our African-American brothers and sisters."[24] This kind of language triggers immediate responses from the Alt-Right, even those that identify as Christian. Hunter Wallace, for example, described Russell Moore, the current president of the Ethics and Religious Liberty Commission of the SBC, as an "anti-Southern cultural maggot."[25]

Supporters of the Alt-Right, as well as many mainstream conservatives, are also critical of the current pope. The Argentinean Pope Francis, the first non-European pope in more than one thousand years and the first pope ever from the Southern Hemisphere, has focused on very different issues than those that animate America's political right. Whereas Pope John Paul II was a consistent ally of the United States on the issue of communism and beloved by conservatives as a result, Pope Francis's view of Islamic terrorism is decidedly different from the views typically put forward by conservatives. For example, Pope Francis does not apparently share the typical conservative view on Islam. He has denounced Islamophobia on multiple occasions.[26]

Abortion is one of the few subjects that conservative Catholics and Protestants have not wavered on. Both the Vatican and the major evangelical denominations remain committed to the prolife cause. But in the eyes of many on the Alt-Right, this intransigence is a problem, not an asset. Although not unified in their opinion, the Alt-Right, on average, is more prochoice than the mainstream conservative movement. This is not because the Alt-Right is committed to a woman's right to choose. Instead, many on the Alt-Right favor abortion because they believe it is eugenic. Although conservatives often argue that abortion is racist because a disproportionate number of abortions take place within the African American and Hispanic communities, many voices on the Alt-Right look at those same numbers and declare abortion a good thing. As one Alt-Right essayist put it:

> First of all, the pro-life position is clearly dysgenic. A 2011 study showed that in 2008, while 16 percent of women aged 15–44 lived below the poverty line, among women

> who had abortions, the number was 42 percent. Hispanic and African-American women made up a combined 31 percent of this age group, but almost 55 percent of those who chose to terminate a pregnancy. The reasons behind these patterns aren't hard to figure out. In a world with reliable birth control, it is quite easy to avoid an unwanted pregnancy; the only ones who can't are the least intelligent and responsible members of society: women who are disproportionately Black, Hispanic, and poor.[27]

Given all of the above, it is no surprise that the Alt-Right has furiously attacked the major leaders and institutions of Christianity. Yet, as I see it, the Alt-Right also seems to be becoming less overtly hostile to Christianity as such—*The Right Stuff*, for example, recently began hosting an Alt-Right Christian podcast called "The Godcast." It is now easy to find many Alt-Right bloggers and other figures that identify as Christians while still denouncing mainstream politicized Christianity.

I asked Gregory Hood about this. Hood is a prolific Alt-Right essayist and the author of the book *Waking Up from the American Dream*.[28] He is also well known as a non-Christian and has written multiple essays on paganism and religion in general.[29] According to Hood, within the Alt-Right

> there is actually more of a tendency moving back towards Christianity. However, this "Christianity" is of a form deeply hostile towards most recognized Christian authorities today, guys like Pope Francis, Russell Moore, etc. Everyone on the Alt Right agrees contemporary Christian leaders have essentially betrayed their own flock. Where there is a difference is whether they believe

this is inherent to Christianity or whether contemporary Christian leaders are essentially heretics.[30]

CASES OF ALT-RIGHT HARASSMENT OF CONSERVATIVES

The Alt-Right has no fond feelings for the mainstream conservative movement or its primary spokespersons. However, not all conservatives have been attacked by the Alt-Right with equal fervor. Some individuals have been targeted directly by the Alt-Right, suffering incessant harassment (usually online but occasionally in the real world) and "doxing"—the release of personal information such as their home addresses and phone numbers. In 2016, there were two primary catalysts for an Alt-Right attack on a conservative: articles or spoken statements against the Alt-Right and opposition to Donald Trump. Jewish conservatives were especially likely to be targeted.

Among the Alt-Right's conservative critics, no one has been more vocal and forceful than the Republican strategist Rick Wilson. During an interview about Donald Trump on MSNBC, Wilson raised the subject of the Alt-Right:

> The screamers and crazy people on the Alt-Right, as they call it, who love Donald Trump, who have plenty of Hitler iconography in their Twitter icons, who think Donald Trump is the greatest thing, oh, it's something, but the fact of the matter is that most of them are childless single men who masturbate to anime. They're not real political players. They're not people who matter in the overall course of humanity.[31]

He later described them as "the saddest individuals in the world."[32] It is thus not surprising that Wilson became a target for Alt-Right threats and insults. An entire 4chan thread was dedicated to Wilson, and a harassment campaign began against him, including sending materials to his home address. He even reported threats to his daughter's safety.[33]

Wilson continued to downplay the Alt-Right even as the attacks increased, but other conservative targets were more alarmed. David French, who was among the first conservatives to denounce the Alt-Right publicly (he was also a vocal opponent of Donald Trump, enough so that for a time he was promoted as a possible conservative third-party candidate), was another subject of frequent Alt-Right attacks. In the eyes of the Alt-Right, French is particularly problematic because he and his wife had adopted a child from Africa. Wilson described some of the abuse he and his family received on social media:

> I distinctly remember the first time I saw a picture of my then-seven-year-old daughter's face in a gas chamber. It was the evening of September 17, 2015. I had just posted a short item to the Corner calling out notorious Trump ally Ann Coulter for aping the white-nationalist language and rhetoric of the so-called alt-right. Within minutes, the tweets came flooding in. My youngest daughter is African American, adopted from Ethiopia, and in alt-right circles that's an unforgivable sin. It's called "race-cucking" or "raising the enemy."[34]

French also described e-mails sent directly to his wife, including one threatening her with "the business end of a gun."[35]

Although, as of this writing, I am aware of no violence in the real world that has occurred as a result of these online campaigns, many conservatives have openly worried that these threats could escalate into real-world danger. In an article in the *New York Times*, Erickson described encounters with Trump supporters on his doorstop.[36] Erickson's son was also harassed in a public place because of his father's opposition to Trump. Bethany Mandel, a conservative columnist, was sufficiently alarmed by these threats to purchase a firearm.[37] Describing her drastic decision, Mandel said:

> After the South Carolina primary, I made an offhand remark on Twitter about Trump's legions of anti-Semitic fans. It wasn't my first time commenting on this; I've even written about the phenomenon in these pages. But the response was unlike anything I've seen before on Twitter. I was called a "slimy Jewess" and told that I "deserve the oven." Not only was the anti-Semitic deluge scary and graphic, it got personal. Trump fans began to "dox" me — a term for adversaries' attempt to ferret out private or identifying information online with malicious intent. My conversion to Judaism was used as a weapon against me, and I received death threats in my private Facebook mailbox, prompting me to file a police report.[38]

Conservatives harassed by the Alt-Right do not have a clear solution. They can simply ignore the abuse, following the maxim that engaging with a troll encourages more trolling. But that seems to preclude speaking out against a movement will not go away on its own. Matt Lewis, when I asked him about this, answered:

At the micro level, I generally do ignore them. The adage "Don't feed the trolls" is generally true. These people crave attention. On the macro level, however, I think it's important to go on the record exposing and confronting evil. So I have used my small perch to publicly condemn this movement, while generally ignoring their personal attacks.[39]

WHY CONSERVATIVES HAVE FAILED (SO FAR) TO DEFEAT THE ALT-RIGHT

Since they first became aware of the Alt-Right, mainstream conservatives have been discussing ways to deal with this phenomenon. Over the last sixty years, conservatives have a strong track record of purging the right of its most dangerous elements—anti-Semites, racists, conspiracy theorists, etc. Thus, one could reasonably believe that conservatives could similarly drive the Alt-Right from public view.

The conservative movement is quick to claim that the most damaging charges that the left makes against conservatives (that they are sexist, racist, anti-Semitic, or just paranoid and crazy in a general sense) are unfounded and unfair. There are, however, times when the conservative elites will agree with the left that a group or individual on the right may be accurately labeled with some or all of those terms. Mainstream conservatives will then declare that this group or movement has no place in public discourse. I documented the history of these conservative purges in *Right-Wing Critics*[40] so do not need to dwell on this issue in detail here. But the periodic housecleaning of conservative institutions usually follows this pattern: when the leaders of the movement determine that an individual or group has become inconvenient, embarrassing, or dangerous, it responds by making a short-term alliance with the left and the political center in order to exile the apostates from public life.

This has occurred multiple times throughout American political history since the birth of the conservative movement. An early example was the conservative attack on the John Birch Society, which proved a hindrance to conservatism because of the anticommunist paranoia of its leader, Robert Welch. Conservatives also energetically responded to the surprising popularity of the white nationalist David Duke in Louisiana, insisting that his ideas were not conservative and that he had no place in the movement. Mainstream conservatives also eventually distanced themselves from Patrick Buchanan and his brand of paleoconservatism. There have been many purges of journalists, intellectuals, and pundits: Joseph Sobran, Sam Francis, and John Derbyshire all once wrote for mainstream conservative publications but were fired when they expressed explicitly racist or anti-Semitic sentiments. These occasional purges remind those within the movement that there are consequences for crossing certain boundaries. Over time, these boundaries shift, and rhetoric that would have been considered mainstream at one point becomes unspeakable within a few decades; for examples of this, we can compare what *National Review* was saying about the issues of race and segregation in the 1960s to what it is saying today. The magazine that declared that "the South must prevail" against those fighting desegregation in 1957 promoted what it called "Civil Rights Republicanism" in 2016.[41]

When it came to defining the boundaries of conservatism and keeping right-wing heretics out of the public eye, William

F. Buckley played, by far, the most important role. He was critical in the demonization of Welch and the John Birch Society and similarly important in keeping Ayn Rand's objectivist movement on the margins of conservative intellectual life.[42] His influence kept Mel Bradford from being appointed the head of the National Endowment for Humanities during the Reagan administration, and he was an early and important conservative voice denouncing David Duke. As Patrick Buchanan was reaching the peak of his influence, Buckley dedicated an entire issue of *National Review* to considering whether Buchanan (and Buckley's own colleague Joseph Sobran) were anti-Semites, concluding that they were.

When the Alt-Right made waves, conservatives were quick to call for a new purge. As Jonah Goldberg put it in an interview with Hugh Hewitt: "As William F. Buckley led the effort to drive the Birchers out of the party, so must genuine conservatives drive out what you and I agree is the core alt right."[43] Unfortunately for conservatives and others distressed by the Alt-Right's new online prominence, it is unclear what such an effort would look like. There are three reasons to doubt that future conservative attacks on the Alt-Right will be successful: the current state of American conservatism, the changing nature of communication, and the nature of the Alt-Right.

At present, the conservative movement is on its heels. The failure of the conservative intelligentsia to stop Donald Trump in the GOP primaries demonstrated the movement's weakness. As of this writing, the organized conservative movement is at the nadir of its influence, despite the GOP's present electoral dominance.

The conservative movement's evolving attitude toward Trump shows how much its influence has waned. Since Trump's election, major conservative institutions have tried to make peace with him and his movement, downplaying the degree to which Trump is not a movement conservative. We saw this new conciliatory approach to Trump on display at the 2016 Conservative Political Action Conference (CPAC), the most important annual gathering of conservative activists and leaders. In 2015, Trump turned down the opportunity to speak at the event when it was clear that he would not face a friendly audience.[44] This was an obvious snub to the conservative movement and a break with Republican convention; historically, GOP presidential contenders do not turn down opportunities to address CPAC. Conservative feelings toward Trump were demonstrated by his abysmal performance in the conference straw poll—he came in distant third, behind Ted Cruz and Marco Rubio. Yet in 2016, Trump was the event's keynote speaker, and anti-Trump sentiments were not expressed on any of the stages.

National Review dedicated an entire issue to denouncing Trump in early 2016. The contributors to the symposium accused him of being both a liberal and a racist.[45] Hitler's name was brought up three times in the issue.[46] The magazine has had a different tone since Trump's election. Although the editors have not rescinded their earlier critiques of Trump, they have started publishing articles with Trumpian themes. Before the election, writers at *National Review* denounced nationalism.[47] In 2017, the magazine published a cover story titled "For Love of Country: A Defense of Nationalism."[48]

Earlier Republican presidents felt it necessary to kiss the rings of leading conservative journalists and intellectuals and promise to be guided by conservative principles. Trump refused to do so and won the election without their assistance. Many conservatives have since maintained their anti-Trump stance, insisting that Trump cannot be considered a true conservative and is thus unworthy of their support.[49] But for the duration of his presidency, Trump will determine the course of the Republican Party, and conservatives that refuse to associate with him will be irrelevant. As Harry Cheadle noted in *Vice*:

> Some conservatives complained about [Trump's CPAC] speech on Twitter, but there's nothing the movement's writers and intellectuals can do. Trump proved he doesn't need them, while they obviously need him very badly in order to get their agenda passed. All those years conservatives spent amassing political power and creating an alternative media universe paid off, they won—except in the process their entire apparatus was taken over by an unpredictable orange reality TV show star. And the kicker is it turns out the rank and file on the right actually like him a lot better than anyone the GOP has given them.[50]

The changing media landscape creates other problems for conservatism. While the conservative purging mechanism still appears to be relatively strong—there are recent examples of individuals that were fired or shut out of certain publications after their deviation from the conservative party line, especially for crossing a line on racial issues[51]—the proliferation of new right-wing publications on the Internet means that such people can still reach an audience with relative ease. So while the Internet is a new avenue for spreading the conservative message, it is an avenue that other voices can take advantage of as well. The Internet has no gate and thus no gatekeepers. The old sources of conservative thought no longer have a monopoly on the means of right-wing communication, and it is now easier than ever for interested readers and listeners to access dissident views.

The third challenge to purging has to do with the Alt-Right's own stance toward the conservative movement. Over the last sixty years, most of the right-wing groups and individuals purged from the conservative movement, and by extension from public discourse, *wanted* to be part of the organized conservative movement. The John Birch Society did not reject the basic premises of conservatism; it was purged because it was embarrassing. David Duke ran as a generic Republican who happened to be openly racist. Pat Buchanan was certainly critical of the organized conservative movement, but he did not reject conservatism as such. Many of the writers who were cast aside by the mainstream conservative publications would probably have been happy to continue to write for such venues had they been allowed to do so.

Unfortunately for the conservative movement, the Alt-Right is of a different opinion. The Alt-Right is not interested in a seat at the conservative table. Many white racist movements in the United States could be described as simply more racist versions of conservatism; the Alt-Right, on the other hand, rejects most of the basic principles of the conservative movement. Beyond the conservative movement's self-declared devotion to color-blind politics, the Alt-Right also rejects the religious right, is skeptical of global capitalism, and has zero interest in early conservative classic texts. The Alt-Right genuinely and openly wants to see the conservative movement destroyed; thus being denied ink and pixels from *Commentary* is no threat of any kind.

To some extent, asking conservatives to "purge" the Alt-Right is akin to asking the United Methodist Church to purge the homophobic Westboro Baptist Church from American life. The two are completely separate, and the people carrying signs declaring "God hates fags" have no interest in what the Methodists think of them. Alt-Right supporters, similarly, do not care what Ross Douthat thinks of them. Conservatives have no way to purge these people. Instead they must persuade present and possible Alt-Right supporters that their reasonable conservative vision is superior to the vision of the Alt-Right.

CONCLUSION

The Alt-Right may ultimately create a new fondness among progressives for the conservatism they have battled over the last six decades. Although conservatives and liberals have spent the last several generations engaged in brutal political combat, both ideologies shared important premises. Although conservatives did not rank equality as the most important political value, most did not openly reject equality entirely—this could not be done without also rejecting the words in the Declaration of Independence. The religious right, similarly, was long a hindrance to major progressive victories, especially on cultural issues, but some Christian leaders have recently started to support traditionally progressive causes.

With conservatism in a weakened state, right-wing currents that have long been out of view are beginning to show themselves. Whether the Alt-Right has a long-term future remains to be seen, but if conservatism ultimately breaks down, other right-wing movements will arise and continue to battle the left. In the long run, progressives may find that the mainstream conservative movement was a less menacing opponent than whatever replaces it.

5

THE ALT-RIGHT AND THE 2016 ELECTION

At the start of 2015, few could have guessed that a movement like the Alt-Right would be a significant part of the story of the 2016 election. The campaign that many anticipated, in which Hillary Clinton engaged in civil debates with Jeb Bush, Marco Rubio, or John Kasich, did not materialize. Ted Cruz was supposed to be the most outrageous figure in the Republican primaries, and few expected him to perform particularly well. Donald Trump's successful campaign sowed disorder in American politics, and this produced an opening the Alt-Right was able to exploit successfully.

The first incarnation of the Alt-Right had little interest in electoral politics, and before the announcement of his presidential run, the far right paid little attention to Trump, even as he made outlandish claims about President Obama's birth certificate. However, when he kicked off his campaign with references to Mexicans as rapists and drug dealers and made a southern border wall the centerpiece of his early speeches, the Alt-Right believed it had finally found its champion. The rise of Donald Trump in the polls and the proliferation of the

#altright hashtag grew in tandem. Trump became the main focus of the Alt-Right on social media. And when Trump's opponents tied Trump directly to the Alt-Right, the movement received unprecedented attention.

Most of the Alt-Right realized from the beginning that Trump was not really one of them, but they still loved him, and not just because of his comments about immigrants and Muslims. Trump changed the tone of American politics. He regularly violated conventions and helped normalize nativist rhetoric. Perhaps most importantly and exciting for those in the Alt-Right, Trump dealt the organized conservative movement a devastating blow, creating an opening for right-wing alternatives.

WHY THE ALT-RIGHT LOVED TRUMP

Let me emphasize that Trump's ideology (if it can even be called an ideology) is not the same as the Alt-Right's. In spite of the hyperbole of some of his opponents and some of his Alt-Right supporters, Trump is not a fascist, a Nazi, or a white nationalist. Building a border wall may be bad policy, but such a policy proposal is hardly exceptional among Republicans—even John McCain called for a border fence in a television ad.[1] Although Trump and the Alt-Right share a certain rhetorical coarseness, the Alt-Right is most definitely far to Trump's right. I will further clarify why I make this distinction in the pages ahead.

If Trump cannot be accurately defined as a white nationalist, what explains his particular appeal to the Alt-Right? He is obviously not the first Republican to lambast undocumented immigration. If being a hard-line immigration skeptic is all it takes for a Republican to generate massive enthusiasm on the far right, why was the radical right not similarly enthused about Tom Tancredo when he ran for president in 2008? If dog-whistle racism is sufficient to garner massive support from open racists, where was the groundswell of white-nationalist excitement for George H. W. Bush after the infamous Willie Horton advertisement in 1988?[2] There is clearly some other dynamic at work, one that makes Trump different from other Republicans.

The main difference with Trump—and likely his greatest gift to the Alt-Right—was that he created chaos in American politics. By taking on the established elites in both the conservative movement and the Republican Party, he ended the conservative monopoly on right-wing politics. He showed that the right could win without following the game plan that had been crafted by Republican elites.

In the years before the 2016 election, the Republican Party's leadership wanted to move away from the party's traditional restrictionist immigration stance, both because such a stance is at odds with important elements of the existing Republican coalition and because the party hoped to expand its support among Latinos and other demographic groups that were turned off by anti-immigrant rhetoric. Following Mitt Romney's loss in the 2012 presidential election, a report commissioned by the Republican National Committee called on the party to embrace liberalizing immigration reforms in order to reach out to new voter blocs.[3]

Trump's popularity dashed all hope that the GOP could shed its reputation for nativism. He showed that rank-and-file Republican voters wanted border walls, not a pathway to citizenship for undocumented immigrants. Although Trump's views on Islam and immigration are not the same as the Alt-Right's, he made them a key part of the national conversation at a time when Republican leaders hoped to focus on important (but less racially charged) issues such as tax cuts, health care, and deregulation. The Alt-Right was quick to realize the opportunity that the Trump campaign presented, and it made the 2016 presidential election the focus of its online activities.

As the GOP primaries progressed, Trump maintained his restrictionist immigration position and attacked fellow Republicans like John McCain, and the Alt-Right focused its energies on promoting Trump, trolling his opponents, and ratcheting up the polarization in what was already a heated campaign. Memes of Trump depicted as a grandiose emperor figure became ubiquitous on Alt-Right social media.

While enthusiastic about Trump, there was a general recognition among white nationalists that Trump did not ultimately share their worldview. For that reason, some on the Alt-Right suggested that their movement be cautious about being too enthusiastic about Trump. Matt Parrot, who is best known for promoting an amalgamation of white nationalism and Orthodox Christianity, said early in the campaign: "While there's an understandable impulse to rally behind a powerful man who shares our vision, Donald Trump is only standing behind one sliver of our total vision, and he's only been doing it for a few weeks. Until a powerful man emerges who truly and completely shares our vision, we should resist the urge to endorse or support any man."[4]

Although white nationalists usually recognize that Trump does not endorse their views, many have expressed gratitude to Trump for moving the direction of the national conversation in a more right-wing direction, creating space for their ideas. As Greg Johnson said: "Like an icebreaker, Trump has plowed through the frozen crust of the artificial political consensus, smashing it to bits and releasing the turbulent populist currents beneath. It is our job to crowd into the breach, widen it, and turn every outcome in our direction."[5] The metaphor of Trump as an ideological icebreaker is apparently popular on the radical right; Richard Spencer has made the same comparison.[6]

The Trump phenomenon was sufficiently important to the Alt-Right for the National Policy Institute to host an entire conference in Washington, D.C., dedicated to the subject in March 2016. In a conversation with reporters covering the event, Spencer again reiterated that Trump has been a boon to the Alt-Right: "I think Trump has opened up some space just in being—going after P.C., liberal gatekeepers, with just a lot of gusto."[7] There was no evidence that the Trump campaign had any role in this event, and no representatives from the campaign commented on the conference.

To examine the Alt-Right's focus on the Trump campaign, in late spring of 2016, as the GOP primaries were coming to an end, I downloaded twenty thousand Tweets that included the Alt-Right hashtag and looked at the frequency with which certain terms appeared. After deleting neutral common words ("and," "the," etc.), I generated a word cloud, which shows the seventy-five most common words in Alt-Right-related tweets. Larger words are those that appeared with greater frequency.

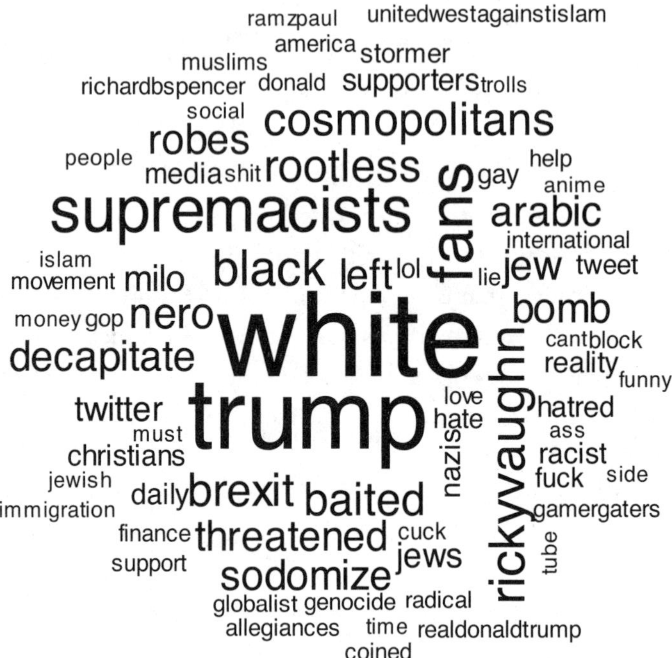

In the word cloud, we see immediately that "white" was, by a wide margin, the most common term. After that, however, "Trump" was the second most common term. This word cloud also demonstrates the Alt-Right's fondness for profanity. Not all of the profanity comes from those who associate with the Alt-Right, however. A significant minority of Twitter users who use the hashtag are opponents of the movement and use strong language to denounce the Alt-Right. Some of these terms will only be familiar to people with some knowledge of the Alt-Right. "Ramzpaul," for example, is the screen name of a popular Alt-Right video blogger.[8] And "Nero" was Milo Yiannopoulos's Twitter username before he was banned from the platform.

Whether Trump had ever even heard of the Alt-Right at the start of the campaign is unknown. However, Trump did interact with some Alt-Right accounts on Twitter and was criticized for it. For example, on one occasion Trump retweeted a picture posted by a user with the Twitter handle "White GenocideTM," although the tweet itself did not have any racist content.[9] There was widespread condemnation of Trump for sharing this Tweet, though it was also clear that many people did not really understand the "white genocide" reference; when white nationalists use that phrase online, they typically mean that whites are in the process of suffering a genocide, not that they should conduct one of their own. Trump also once retweeted a drawing of himself depicted as Pepe, though again it is unclear if he understood what this meant at the time.[10]

Trump has also retweeted comments from people who are ideologically aligned with the Alt-Right.[11] These casual interactions on Twitter have both excited radical rightists and raised additional concerns from mainstream commentators about Trump.

TRUMP'S OPPONENTS MADE THE ALT-RIGHT PART OF THE NATIONAL CONVERSATION

The Alt-Right made significant waves in 2015 and early 2016, getting the attention of major journalists. But even during that time many people outside the movement, even those who followed politics closely, were ignorant of the Alt-Right. This changed in the summer preceding the election, when Hillary Clinton directly attacked the Alt-Right in a major speech, declaring it a significant player in the campaign. Clinton did not just make a passing reference to the Alt-Right; it was the primary theme of the speech. The catalyst for the speech was

Trump's decision to hire Stephen Bannon, who will be discussed in more detail in the next chapter. In the speech, Clinton provided a brief description of the Alt-Right:

> This is not conservatism as we have known it. This is not Republicanism as we have known it. These are race-baiting ideas, anti-Muslim and anti-immigrant ideas, anti-woman——all key tenets making up an emerging racist ideology known as the "Alt-Right."
>
> Now Alt-Right is short for "Alternative Right."
>
> The *Wall Street Journal* describes it as a loose but organized movement, mostly online, that "rejects mainstream conservatism, promotes nationalism and views immigration and multiculturalism as threats to white identity."[12]

These lines further demonstrate the weirdness of the 2016 presidential election. Few would have expected Clinton, just months before the election, to attack her opponent for failing to be a conservative, thus implicitly defending conservatism and "Republicanism as we have known it." Both Clintons had fought conservatives for decades. Yet she went on to praise George W. Bush, long a despised figure on the left, for his tolerant approach toward Muslims and lauded John McCain's 2008 presidential campaign, stating, "We need that kind of leadership again."[13] Indeed, in these appeals she seemed to be aiming her speech at Republicans with misgivings about Trump rather than her own progressive base, which needed no additional reasons to dislike Trump. By tying Trump to the Alt-Right, it appears Clinton was trying to drive a wedge between traditional conservatives and the GOP's new standard bearer. At the time, this seemed like a sound strategy. As Michelle Goldberg noted in *Slate*:

> It's hard to say how Republican officials will respond. Most of them hate the alt-right, which denigrates them as pathetic cuckservatives. But Clinton succeeded in tying Trump to the alt-right in a way that will make it hard to disavow one without the other. Trump, meanwhile, will be tempted to lash out, lest it look as if he'd been intimidated by a woman he derides as weak and frail. His response, so far, was to tweet: "Just watched recap of #CrookedHillary's speech. Very short and lies. She is the only one fear-mongering!" In fact, the speech could have been twice as long; there's enough material. But it was long enough to define Trump and his most fervent followers as people beyond the pale of American politics.[14]

Many of Trump's conservative opponents agreed that this was a sound strategy. Following the speech, Matt Lewis stated, "Hillary is doing EXACTLY what she should."[15] Amanda Carpenter, a conservative political commentator, declared on Twitter, "This speech has to be making Trump surrogates squirm. Yes, this is what you signed up to defend."[16] Carpenter reiterated this point the next day:

> Had Trump not hired Bannon, Clinton would not have given that speech. There would have been no clear and direct link between the Trump campaign and the Alt-Right. As of last week, they are fused.
>
> With Bannon, the Alt-Right is literally running the Trump campaign. And, many Republican voters can

> now reasonably say, "Yes, I am Republican, but I'm not one of them. I'm not Alt-Right. I don't have to support Donald Trump."
>
> Clinton couldn't have asked Trump to make a better hire to help her campaign.[17]

Although Clinton brought the Alt-Right to the attention of people who would not otherwise have known of the movement, certain elements of her speech were more confusing than clarifying. For example, although the speech was billed as being about the Alt-Right, she spent a portion of her time discussing Alex Jones and his relationship with Trump. Alex Jones is a famous conspiracy theorist known for making outlandish claims, but he is not associated with the Alt-Right. His claims about conspiracies and cover-ups (arguing that events like 9/11 and the Oklahoma City Bombing were "inside jobs") certainly place him outside the mainstream, but his rants typically lack a racial angle, and Jones has disavowed racism.[18] Although Jones's rhetoric about globalist cabals echoes some sentiments on the Alt-Right (within the Alt-Right, "globalist" is often a code word for Jews), I am aware of no one in the Alt-Right of any significance who has claimed Jones as one of their own.

Clinton also spent much of the speech discussing Trump's connection to Vladimir Putin and Nigel Farage (the former leader of the UK Independence party, or UKIP). Although her statements were all factually correct, it is difficult to say that either of those figures have connections to the Alt-Right in the United States. By expanding the scope of the speech, Clinton implied a more unified radical right-wing movement in support of Trump than probably existed. On this issue, I agree with Tim Stanley's remarks in the *Telegraph:* "So there's a risk of conflating various political projects into some grand movement, and deciding that the whole thing is a coherent conspiracy with a direct line to Trump. The alt-right would love you to think that, as would Hillary Clinton."[19]

Regardless of whether Clinton's speech on the Alt-Right was entirely accurate, the Alt-Right's reaction to the speech was positive. The movement was overjoyed by this new exposure. As a blogger at *TRS* put it: "We in the Alt-Right are thrilled to be receiving so much press, negative or inaccurate as it may be, because it is driving curious people to our cause in droves."[20] A writer at the *Daily Stormer* shared this excitement:

> In the past week, Google searches for "alt-right" have completely exploded, being at least 20x greater than last week.
>
> This, of course, is a result of Hillary's "alt-right speech," as well as the ensuing media storm that followed it. Although this surge is certainly temporary, we can expect an influx of new comers as well in the following days and weeks.[21]

The author of the above quote was correct that interest in the Alt-Right "exploded." Aside from increased web traffic to Alt-Right websites, seemingly every major media venue subsequently published a story on this movement—some providing more accurate portrayals than others. Once this connection had been made, the Alt-Right could justifiably view the subsequent election as being, at least in part, a referendum on the movement. If Trump won, the movement could claim his victory as their own.

THE ALT-RIGHT RESPONSE TO THE RESULTS

As expected, the Alt-Right was jubilant about the results of the 2016 presidential election. Despite consistent polling suggesting a Clinton victory—and perhaps even a Clinton landslide—Trump won an impressive victory in the Electoral College, including several states that no Republican candidate had won in decades. Although it would be a stretch to say that the Alt-Right played a role in Trump's victory (it is possible that Trump's alleged association with the Alt-Right cost him more votes than it gained), the Alt-Right was perhaps Trump's most enthusiastic base of support. The Alt-Right also, perhaps correctly, viewed Trump's election as a fundamental paradigm shift in American politics. As Lawrence Murray said:

> Our position is not unassailable, but it is stronger than ever before. So we celebrate, that President Trump has given rise to nationalism, to America First, to formal recognition of the Alt-Right, to outing cuckservatives as #NeverTrump turncoats, to (((anti-globalist))) memes entering the public consciousness, to levels of shvitzing that shouldn't even be possible, and more than anything else to hope for the future of our people, not just in the United States but around the world. This is as much a victory for White Americans as it is for Swedes, Australians, the British, the French, and other European peoples. We will make the world safe for ethnocracy.[22]

Some voices on the Alt-Right expressed concern, even before the election, that Trump would betray his base and quickly evolve into a more conventional Republican. Some conservatives were hopeful that they would see such an outcome. There were some signs this might occur, such as Trump's decision to name the conventional Republican Reince Priebus as his chief of staff. But shortly after being declared the president-elect, Trump made it clear he was not going to soften his positions, reaffirming his commitment to build a border fence.[23] Trump also had a conversation with Vladimir Putin days after the election, in which Trump apparently expressed his desire to mend relations with Russia,[24] which had become increasingly fraught in recent years after Russian actions in Ukraine and Syria. Just days after his election, Trump reaffirmed his campaign commitments to shut down Muslim immigration by signing an executive order restricting travel from several majority-Muslim countries.[25]

Perhaps more significantly, Trump appointed Steve Bannon as his chief strategist. By selecting Bannon, Trump sent a clear signal that his administration would be fundamentally different from those of his immediate Republican predecessors. Bannon has stated before that he has contempt for much of the mainstream conservative movement; he once described *National Review* and the *Weekly Standard* as "left-wing magazines" and said he "wanted to destroy them."[26]

The Alt-Right entered the mainstream discussion because of the election, and with the election over and the man the Alt-Right called "the god emperor" on his way to the White House, some on the Alt-Right may have been ready to declare victory. But following Trump's win, it was clear that the Alt-Right was not content to rest on its laurels. According to Tory Scot at *The Right Stuff*, "Our goal should be to push Trump as far right as possible, and to encourage him to do as much damage to the enemies of white America as he can, while at the same time doing all we can to agitate the left into an anti-white frenzy. Make them alienate would be sympathizers."[27]

The reality is that Donald Trump's win may have done little to advance the Alt-Right's agenda. Thus, the Alt-Right was determined to continue to push the boundaries of what was acceptable in American political discourse. To quote one Alt-Right essayist:

> So, yes, it is good that Donald Trump won, and I have been hearing talk on the Alt Right about whites now having a decade or two of breathing room in order to fend off their own demographic demise. We should not think that way. Until proven otherwise, we should consider a Trump presidency as little more than a hiccup on this tragic slide to white irrelevance. A four-year-long, scandal-filled, orange and blonde hiccup. We need such a pessimistic view of Donald Trump because only a pessimistic view of Donald Trump will animate white, race-realist Right-wingers in the Alt Right to grab a Trump administration by its red tie and shake it until it does what we want it to do. In other words, we are not outsiders anymore. Trump's victory has cracked open the window through which we can become insiders again. We need to slam that window open and make our presence felt.[28]

TRUMP (AND HIS ADVISORS) SHOULD NOT BE CLASSIFIED AS ALT-RIGHT

Given the tremendous enthusiasm the Alt-Right showed for Trump in 2016, it made sense for opponents of both Trump and the Alt-Right to point out connections between the two.

But I think it is an exaggeration to say that Trump is part of the Alt-Right.

Beyond his statements and actions regarding Mexicans and Muslims, Trump has been tied to the Alt-Right mainly because of who he has named his closest advisors. Steve Bannon is the most significant of these figures. Before being named as the Trump campaign's CEO, Bannon ran the conservative website *Breitbart* (named after the late Andrew Breitbart, a conservative writer and activist). Bannon once explicitly described *Breitbart* as a "platform of the alt-right."[29] Although I can only speculate why Bannon would make such a claim, the reality is that this statement is incorrect. No figure at *Breitbart* has ever explicitly endorsed white nationalism. It is true that *Breitbart* is a right-wing webzine, was for many years home to Milo Yiannopoulos, and has published many negative articles about immigrants, Muslims, feminists, and racial and ethnic minorities. But these articles have differed more in tone than in substance from what you can find in more mainstream conservative magazines and websites. At most, *Breitbart* can be broadly categorized as part of the so-called Alt-Lite, which I will discuss in the next chapter. The Alt-Right is clear in its belief that nonwhites should be excluded from majority-white countries precisely because they are nonwhite. No article at *Breitbart* has ever, to my knowledge, openly made such a statement. Like Trump, Bannon is a right-wing nationalist and a populist, which sets him apart from traditional conservatives, but as of this writing, the evidence that he is a white nationalist is weak.

Stephen Miller, who joined the Trump campaign in early 2016 and is now a key figure in the Trump administration, has also been tied to the Alt-Right. This connection has some plausibility, as Miller, who currently serves as a senior advisor to the president for policy, attended Duke University at the same time as Richard Spencer (Miller was an undergraduate and Spencer was a graduate student), and the two worked together to sponsor a debate on immigration, which included Peter Brimelow of VDare.com as one of the speakers.[30] Spencer has even praised Miller's work for Trump, declaring that he "is much tougher than any cuck."[31] And before joining the Trump campaign, Miller worked for Jeff Sessions (R-Ala.), who was consistently one of the most outspoken anti-immigration voices in the U.S. Senate.

Based on this, one could make a circumstantial case that Miller has certain Alt-Right inclinations. Yet I remain hesitant to label Miller as part of the Alt-Right. In the eyes of much of the Alt-Right, the fact that Miller is Jewish precludes him from being part of the movement. Spencer himself has declared that Miller "is not a white nationalist or an identitarian."[32] In a later article, Spencer dismissed the claim that he was an important mentor to Miller, stating, "I hope I influenced Stephen, as I hope I influence everyone I come into contact with. That said, Stephen is his own man, and we have different political philosophies."[33] For his part, Miller denied that he is friends with Spencer, declaring, "I strongly condemn his views."[34]

Notable conservatives have come to Miller's defense against the charge that he is part of the Alt-Right, arguing that Miller's ideological moorings are closer to those of David Horowitz (a conservative writer) than of Spencer.[35] This is also controversial, given that Horowitz is arguably one of the most Islamophobic mainstream conservative voices in America.[36] But Horowitz's positions are also distinct from those of the Alt-Right; as I argued in chapter 1, a single-minded focus on the purported dangers of Muslim immigration, rather than nonwhite immigration more generally, is more common among conservatives than it is among the Alt-Right. Finally, I can find no evidence that any significant figure in the Alt-Right besides Spencer even knew who Miller was before he joined the Trump campaign. It is possible that there is more to the story than what is now publicly available, but until there is additional evidence suggesting otherwise, I feel safe concluding that Miller has had no meaningful association with the Alt-Right since the concept was born.

One may argue that I am whitewashing the Trump administration and downplaying its radicalism. This is not my intention. Trump represents a major deviation from the mainstream conservatism of Ronald Reagan or George W. Bush. His views and actions on immigration are far to the right of what used to be the mainstream within the Republican Party. But saying that Trump and the Alt-Right are simpatico amounts to whitewashing the Alt-Right. The Alt-Right wants more than an end to undocumented immigration or to receiving refugees from majority-Muslim countries; it wants nonwhites out of the country, whether they are immigrants or not, even if they can trace their ancestry back to the colonial period. One does not need to be a pro-Trump partisan to see a categorical difference between his policies and those pushed by the Alt-Right.

An analogy may better explain my point. If the outcome of the 2016 election had been very different, with Senator Bernie Sanders defeating Hillary Clinton in the primary and Donald Trump in the general election, he would have represented a new variety of Democrat in the White House, one far to the left of recent Democrats. He also would have been a president whose campaign enjoyed enthusiastic support from the small number of contemporary American Maoists.[37] Yet if

Sanders's conservative opponents claimed that the new president was a Maoist and swore he was on the verge of implementing his own version of the Great Leap Forward, they would be justifiably ridiculed for their hyperbole. Just as it is not a defense of Sanders's economic platform to say he is not a Maoist, it is not a defense of Trump's policies on race and immigration to say he is not part of the Alt-Right.

I recognize that some will remain unsatisfied with my argument, and a number of talented and respected writers have argued that the Trump administration is in fact a white-nationalist regime.[38] I think this claim is mistaken. More importantly, I believe clarity and precision in language are useful, and the overuse of terms such as "fascist," "Nazi," and "white supremacist" hinder productive political discussions. This was a problem long before Trump became a political figure. George W. Bush was frequently compared to Adolf Hitler;[39] the conservative columnist Jonah Goldberg wrote a best-selling book arguing that modern progressivism was disturbingly similar to fascism.[40] In my view, both of these comparisons are absurd. More importantly, this kind of rhetoric tends to shut down conversation; few reasonable people will care to engage with an ideologue that casually smears his or her political opponents as Nazis. Trump's variety of right-wing populism can be forcefully critiqued without resorting to sensationalist bombast.

There is simply no evidence that Trump or any significant figure in the White House desires the mass expulsion of all nonwhites from all or part of the United States, which is the core belief of white nationalists. Trump and his administration can and should be criticized for their actual statements and policies. But inflating the significance of tenuous connections between the White House and the Alt-Right is potentially dangerous. Declaring that Trump's entire movement represents white nationalism makes it difficult rhetorically to disentangle the Alt-Right from the rest of Trump's supporters, most of whom do not share the Alt-Right's core beliefs.

THE POSTELECTION CONTROVERSY

The Alt-Right's jubilation following Trump's victory was short-lived. The movement faced new controversies and an even greater amount of mainstream-media hostility following a postelection NPI conference that occurred on November 19, 2016. Like American Renaissance conferences, NPI conferences are typically disciplined affairs, where smartly dressed, articulate speakers promote their message in front of a polite audience using careful language. This was true for most of this NPI conference, as well.[41] The tone changed at the end of the conference, however, when Spencer gave his concluding speech. Abandoning the calm, soft-spoken tones that are the norm at these kinds of events, Spencer opted for more inflammatory, grandiose language. As his speech was coming to a close, Spencer declared:

> As Europeans, we are, uniquely, at the center of history. We are, as Hegel recognized, the concept of world history. No one will honor us for losing gracefully. No one mourns the great crimes committed against us. For us, it is conquer or die. This is a unique burden for the white man, that our fate is entirely in our hands. And it is appropriate because within us, within the very blood in our veins as children of the sun lies the potential for greatness.

> That is the great struggle we are called to. We were not meant to live in shame and weakness and disgrace. We were not meant to beg for moral validation from some of the most despicable creatures to pollute the soil of this planet. We were meant to overcome—overcome all of it. Because that's natural for us.
>
> Because for us, as Europeans, it's only normal again, when we are great again.[42]

These remarks alone would have generated tremendous controversy. Words like "conquer" only reinforce the view that the Alt-Right really is about white supremacy and the subjugation of nonwhites, and they tend to be eschewed by the racial right's leading voices. But the conference created an even greater scandal as a result of Spencer's concluding statement: "Hail Trump. Hail our people. Hail victory."[43] A minority of the audience responded to this statement by raising their right arm in the Nazi salute. This entire speech, including the audience reaction, was captured on camera by journalists at the *Atlantic*,[44] and over the following week the mainstream media was able to publish and broadcast stories about the Nazi-inspired elements of the conference and the Alt-Right more generally.[45]

Donald Trump's response was even more significant than the media's. Throughout the campaign, Trump had been surprisingly quiet about his support from the Alt-Right, not even denouncing the movement after Hillary Clinton's speech directly tying his presidential run to the Alt-Right. But when presented with material from the NPI conference, Trump immediately stated, "I don't want to energize the group, and I disavow the group."[46] Although significant, I don't want to overstate the importance of this disavowal; after being presented with that footage, it would have been shocking (and politically disastrous) if Trump had not distanced himself from the Alt-Right.

Following the conference, most of the major Alt-Right figures weighed in on the event and the subsequent controversy. Jared Taylor, who spoke earlier in the conference, was quick to condemn the audience reaction to Spencer's speech, declaring in an interview: "I think having some of this attitude as Jews as an enemy, that's not my position at all. I think Jews can very much be white people, men of the west. So I was shocked by these images."[47] Taylor went on, "I was very surprised. I was very saddened by it. I think it's a terrible, terrible pity. I don't endorse any form of National Socialism. I think that's a completely inappropriate and crazy model for the United States."[48]

Other figures on the Alt-Right expressed similar sentiments. The video blogger RamZPaul posted commentary about the conference, stating that "the Alt-Right brand is damaged. It's associated with Nazism. And normal Americans aren't going to support that."[49] At *Counter-Currents*, Greg Johnson said, "It is ironic—or maybe just sadly fitting—that Richard Spencer, the man who launched the Alternative Right brand, may have just destroyed it."[50]

The Alt-Right's response to the conference was not entirely negative, however. The most radical and extreme element of the movement, which had previously been ambivalent about Spencer, was delighted by the speech and the audience response. Writing at the *Daily Stormer*, Andrew Anglin declared:

> As all reading are presumably aware—because we've been covering it nonstop for three days, just like the rest of the media—Richard Spencer gave an absolutely

> fantastic speech at NPI over the weekend at NPI, ending it with a sieg heil to Trump and to the white race.
>
> And the crowd threw up straight armed salutes.
>
> It was glorious.
>
> He named the Jew, as did others at the conference. It was approximately a 9000 point upgrade from previous NPI conferences, which I was personally never thrilled by.[51]

For his part, Richard Spencer was unapologetic. He defended the speech and the audience response by noting that "the Alt Right is boisterous and even outlandish," suggesting that the Nazi salutes were made in a spirit of "irreverence and fun."[52] However, he did acknowledge that these kinds of statements may be unhelpful for the Alt-Right as it attempts to expand its support:

> But we should always remember our goal of reaching that "Eternal Normie"—the people who grasp that something is profoundly wrong with the world . . . but who can't quite articulate it . . . who are looking for a way out . . . and who have been psychologically programmed since birth to see anything related to Nazism as the seat of all evil. In other words, we must demonstrate discipline; this goes for me, as well those who attend public and private events.[53]

At the time of this writing, it is not possible to know whether the NPI speech and the controversy it created will create a long-term problem for the Alt-Right. The event did seem to change how the Alt-Right was discussed in the media.

Shortly after the conference, the Associated Press issued new guidelines on how the Alt-Right should be discussed, declaring that the term should not be used unless readers are also informed what the movement stands for, suggesting that "whenever 'alt-right' is used in a story, be sure to include a definition: 'an offshoot of conservatism mixing racism, white nationalism and populism,' or, more simply, 'a white nationalist movement.' "[54]

CONCLUSION

The Alt-Right was energized by Trump's victory. Trump's position on immigration approximated the Alt-Right's views more than any other Republican nominee's in recent history. His open warfare with the mainstream conservative movement opened a door for more radical right-wing views. The campaign brought the radical right exponentially more media coverage than it had enjoyed in decades. But neither Trump nor his major advisors should be classified as part of the Alt-Right, at least at this point. Even if Donald Trump fulfills his campaign promises to build a border wall and limit Muslim immigration, such policies do not amount to white nationalism.

Although Trump and his leading advisors should not be considered part of the Alt-Right, it is fair to say that they helped push American politics in the Alt-Right's direction. But if the Trump movement can neither be classified as conventionally conservative nor as Alt-Right, some other term is needed, a term for the right-wing populists that got behind Trump but who stop short of the Alt-Right's radicalism. In late 2016, the Alt-Right invented a moniker for people with views that resemble their own in many ways but who typically avoid transparent racism: Alt-Lite. This new category, which includes a much larger number of Trump supporters, is the subject of the next chapter.

6

THE "ALT-LITE"

When the term "Alternative Right" first appeared, it was applied to anyone that fell on the right of the political spectrum but had major problems with the conservative movement. In this broad sense, localists, libertarians, paleoconservatives, right-wing populists, secular conservatives, and white nationalists could all, to some degree, be considered an "alternative right." As Jack Hunter, a libertarian essayist and former staffer to Rand Paul, put it in 2009 (when he was still using the term):

> Though Richard came up with the term "alternative right" I've never thought of it as a label specific to *Taki's Magazine*, Richard Spencer or any individual, but a comprehensive and useful designation for parts of the conservative movement that are both outside the mainstream, yet also philosophically connected, however loosely, primarily due to common ideological ancestors, whether of the libertarian or traditional conservative variety.[1]

Not long after those words were written, it became more obvious that the Alternative Right concept was meant to be a vessel of white-nationalist entryism. This became clearer when Spencer founded the original *Alternative Right* website, which was heavily focused on racial issues. Once this became apparent, the term stopped being used by people who rejected white-identity politics. In fact, for the last year, Hunter has been one of the Alt-Right's more vocal critics on the right.[2]

Yet there was also an important transformation of the Alt-Right throughout 2016. As the term grew in popularity, a larger number of people began to use it, including many that do not apparently desire the creation of a white ethnostate in North America. Because the Alt-Right does not have real leaders in the conventional sense, the movement is able to evolve in various directions, depending on who is using the term and what they think it means. There is no Alt-Right pope with the ability to declare what is or is not an Alt-Right position. As the Alt-Right grew in size, in some ways it seemed to be returning to its original meaning. As the term became more popular, the white-nationalist core of the Alt-Right debated how to treat these new fellow travelers, especially those who do not fully embrace an Alt-Right stance on race and the so-called Jewish Question.

THE GROWTH OF THE "ALT-LITE"

The battle for the Alt-Right's soul was displayed at a speech by Milo Yiannopoulos at the University of Alabama, which was one of the stops on his "Dangerous Faggot Tour" (Yiannopoulos is openly gay). I arrived early to speak with the many young people who were in line for the sold-out event.

Everyone I spoke with had heard of the Alt-Right, and many expressed sympathy and even enthusiasm for the movement. But to my surprise, there was a nearly unanimous insistence among the attendees I spoke with that the Alt-Right has "nothing to do with race." They instead described it as an irreverent assault on political correctness. Perhaps there was an element of social-desirability bias at work: college students, even when assured of their anonymity, may be unlikely to share racist statements with a stranger. But even with that caveat, all of these students seemed sincere.

I was not the only person speaking with attendees in line. People claiming to speak for the *Daily Stormer* were there handing out fliers that condemned Yiannopoulos as a Trojan horse and explained the Alt-Right in this way: "The core concept of the [Alt-Right], upon which all else is based, is that Whites are undergoing an extermination, via mass immigration into White countries which was enabled by a corrosive liberal ideology of White self-hatred, and that the Jewish elites are at the center of this agenda, even Milo himself admitted this."[3] The fliers ended with a link to the *Daily Stormer* website. The neo-Nazi pamphleteers had a point—at present, race is the central element of the Alt-Right.

Yet not everyone who voiced sympathy for the Alt-Right in 2016 was secretly a white nationalist or a neo-Nazi. It seemed that the Alt-Right was still viewed by some as a catch-all term for people with right-wing inclinations who are not interested in the organized conservative movement—thus not all saw or acknowledged the racial component to the Alt-Right. Yiannopoulos suggested as much when I asked him (during the question-and-answer portion of the speech) what his intuition was regarding the size of the Alt-Right. He admitted that he had no idea about the total number. However, he did say the following:

> If you take the broadest possible definition, which is the one I like to use because it's the one that includes the most people who I think are fellow travelers of the movement: resistant to immigration from all sorts of other places, worried about border security, worried about trade, pro-military but anti-intervention overseas, loathing of political correctness. That, whatever you call it, there is obviously a join between cultural libertarianism which my colleague Allum defines as a sort of classical liberalism warmed up by the internet. It contains multitudes I think. And certainly, under my definition of the Alt-Right, a large portion, if not the majority, of Trump support would qualify as Alt-Right.
>
> Now a lot of the key figures in how the Alt-Right started have views that are toward the rightward fringe and resist that. They would rather that the movement was classified more narrowly. And those people tend to be those with slightly more unsavory opinions about things. But I have to look at it as a journalist, as a researcher, as somebody who is called up to give everybody else a definition of this movement. And if a large slice of the population are calling themselves Alt-Right, identifying themselves as Alt-Right, who am I to say they're not? Particularly when it's clear to me that they're all traveling in a broadly similar direction. So I would say that probably all of Donald Trump's supporters under forty, and many of them over forty. And that's why I objected so much to the left—the left was sort of playing along to the extremists, really—the left was trying to define the

> Alt-Right as a sort of hateful, anti-Semitic, misogynistic, racist movement, while at the same time saying that it was huge. It's the Hillary Clinton maneuver, you know? The "basket of deplorables." Well just how many people are in her basket of deplorables? Is it all Donald Trump supporters, and are they, as she suggested, irredeemable? These are extraordinary words to use about vast swaths of the population. I have a feeling that the only thing Hillary Clinton and I would agree on is that the Alt-Right is basically most of Donald Trump's support. We would disagree, of course, on whether or not that's a good thing.[4]

Under Yiannopoulos's definition of the Alt-Right, the term refers to a comparatively innocuous movement that is not particularly different from other right-wing movements we have seen before. Mainstream conservatives have been complaining about political correctness for decades.[5] Concerns about immigration and the border are even more common. Support for trade protectionism and opposition to foreign interventionism are certainly positions at odds with mainstream conservatism, but they are not particularly radical positions.

Although I disagree with Yiannopoulos's definition of the Alt-Right, there is some merit in what he said. There are people with views that broadly correspond with part of the Alt-Right's message but who are not especially racist (or at least do not perceive themselves that way) and who may not be anti-Semitic at all. A new term that appeared in mid-2016 is quite helpful: "Alt-Lite." I am aware of no one who uses the term as a self-description, and is it used as a derogatory term by the Alt-Right. Despite its origin, Alt-Lite is an appropriate description of people whose views on immigration and race relations partially overlap with those on the Alt-Right yet do not cross the line into open white nationalism. According to the Alt-Right, the Alt-Lite recognizes major problems with contemporary American society but is unwilling to accept and declare that these problems can only be resolved via white-identity politics.

Precisely classifying the Alt-Lite and carefully disaggregating this group from the Alt-Right are not straightforward tasks. We can say that the Alt-Lite is more libertarian in its orientation than the Alt-Right. It may believe in biological racial differences but does not necessarily endorse racial separatism. The Alt-Lite believes in the superiority of Western culture and values (including some values, such as tolerance, that many on the Alt-Right reject), but it does not necessarily believe nonwhites are incapable of thriving in Western countries. The Alt-Lite's critique of immigration tends to focus on legality, the question of Islam, and the issue of assimilation. In terms of substance, the Alt-Lite tends to be closer to the Alt-Right than to mainstream conservatives when it comes to immigration. But it stops short of calling for the mass deportation of nonwhites or, at least, those nonwhites that are legally residing in the United States and Europe.

A number of figures have been identified with the Alt-Lite. Some of them have access to major media venues. Yiannopoulos (who has been mistakenly labeled by many media outlets as a "leader of the Alt-Right")[6] was unquestionably the most significant of these throughout 2016, given his large following and willingness to engage openly with and promote the Alt-Right. Yiannopoulos's ideological moorings are ultimately different from the Alt-Right, however. He has, for example, made it very clear that he is not a white nationalist—and as a half-Jewish gay man who claims to have "a very anti-white bedroom policy,"[7] he would probably not find a society based on Alt-Right principles a congenial environment.

That being said, the claim that Yiannopoulos was part of the Alt-Right was not entirely baseless. Even if he is not part of the Alt-Right himself, he did help promote it, and he has downplayed its most radical elements. His 2016 article "An Establishment Conservative's Guide to the Alt-Right," co-authored with Allum Bokhari, remains the most sympathetic portrayal of the movement to appear in a major media venue to date.[8] The article was quite misleading, however, as it suggested that most of the Alt-Right were not sincere racists and were instead saying outrageous things because "it's simply a means to fluster their grandparents."[9] Furthermore, Yiannopoulos's trollish behavior on social media was often reminiscent of what one finds on the Alt-Right. His articles and speeches were no less outrageous. "Feminism is cancer" is one of his catchphrases,[10] and he once gave a speech titled "Ten Things I Hate About Islam."[11] So I should clarify that, although Yiannopoulos is not truly part of the Alt-Right, he is radical and offensive in a way that is often reminiscent of the Alt-Right.

Breitbart, which employed Yiannopoulos until early 2017, may have been properly labeled as an Alt-Lite venue for a time—though, as I will discuss shortly, the site has recently been moving in a more mainstream direction. Although no article at *Breitbart* has ever openly endorsed white nationalism, it has published more incendiary stories about race than one typically finds at mainstream conservative venues.[12] It ran a large number of articles focused specifically on the issue of crimes committed by African Americans, for example.

Gavin McInnes is another figure frequently categorized as Alt-Lite. McInnes also has a large platform and a long career spanning multiple forms of media. Like Yiannopoulos, McInnes initially comes across as someone unlikely to have any affinity for the Alt-Right—he maintains a carefully cultivated hipster persona, and he is married to a Native American woman. He cofounded Vice Media, has starred in multiple movies and television shows, and is a frequent guest on the Fox News Channel. But he has also contributed content to websites affiliated with the Alt-Right. He is a long-time contributor to *Taki's Magazine*, for example, and began writing for that magazine when Richard Spencer was still the editor. He also contributed content to VDare.com, although his last article for that site appears to be more than a decade old. Although I can find no examples of McInnes describing himself as part of the Alt-Right, he continues to correspond with the movement's notable figures and defend them from their critics. He wrote the following in a 2016 *Taki's Magazine* article:

> I'm sure there are bona fide bad guys in America today, but I can't find any. Every time I get face-to-face with someone in the SPLC's "Extremist Files," I meet a reasonable man with a philosophy that is, at the very least, arguable. Jared Taylor is from Japan and says the government should stop funding multiculturalism. Peter Brimelow is an immigrant who thinks immigration in America is a mess. John Derbyshire is a race mixer who loves Jews. Ann Coulter is smart and funny. I've known alt-right pioneer Richard Spencer since he got me the job at this magazine and even he, the head of the snake, comes across as perfectly reasonable in conversation. He doesn't think nonwhites can be included in a harmonious America, but everything else on his plate is relatively civil. These are the bad guys the Antifa [antifascists] is warn-

> ing us about? They sound like the mildest Black Lives Matter activist talking from the bath with a joint in his hand. In fact, the only real villain I can think of is *Daily Stormer*'s Andrew Anglin, but I'm telling you, this guy reeks to high hell of FBI. I can't prove it, but my gut says he and *Daily Stormer* are government fabrications.[13]

A few other names that could be classified as Alt-Lite are Lauren Southern (a Canadian libertarian), Ann Coulter (one of the more bombastic conservative authors and commentators and an early Trump supporter), Mike Cernovich (a pro-Trump blogger), and Paul Joseph Watson (an editor at the conspiracy-theory website *Infowars*). Like the Alt-Right, all of these figures support Trump, attack political correctness, and accuse the mainstream media of dishonesty. But they generally avoid anti-Semitism and the open racism of the Alt-Right.

People bearing the Alt-Lite label are a frequent target of criticism from both the left and the far right. To the Alt-Right, the Alt-Lite is problematic because it threatens to weaken the movement's core message. From the left, they are criticized for normalizing the Alt-Right and helping white nationalism enter the mainstream discussion. That is, by making similar arguments as the Alt-Right but stopping short of calls for white nationalism and generally appearing reasonable, the Alt-Lite may be starting people down a path that ultimately leads them into the ranks of the most radical wing of the Alt-Right. This point has been made by some of the Alt-Right's most aggressive opponents, who accuse the major Alt-Lite voices of mainstreaming certain Alt-Right talking points.[14]

The Alt-Lite, collectively, has a much larger audience than the Alt-Right. Mike Cernovich, Paul Joseph Watson, Lauren Southern, and Gavin McInnes each have over one hundred thousand followers on Twitter, for example—far more than any of the more radical voices on the Alt-Right. Ann Coulter has over one million followers. If even a small percentage of the people who regularly consume Alt-Lite material subsequently move into the Alt-Right camp, then the Alt-Lite will have proved a major boon to its more radical ideological cousin.

THE ALT-RIGHT'S RESPONSE

The arrival of these new, more moderate voices who have expressed sympathy for Alt-Right positions (and are often themselves classified as Alt-Right)[15] created a potential problem for the movement's original supporters. Although the Alt-Right obviously wants to grow, the racialist element does not want to see the movement evolve into mere "edgy" conservatism or libertarianism, to be simply a revival of these other ideologies with the occasional racist joke thrown in the mix. The debate among those within the Alt-Right is whether the more mainstream voices pushing a quasi-Alt-Right message, even in a diluted form, are helping create a new batch of dedicated Alt-Right ideologues.

Some on the Alt-Right want nothing to do with the Alt-Lite. They do not want anyone that is not a hardcore white nationalist to appropriate the term and weaken it. Not surprisingly, Yiannopoulos has been a major target for this element of the Alt-Right. Some of the hostility toward Yiannopoulos stems from his demographic attributes. Some elements of the Alt-Right are also frustrated because he has explicitly downplayed the racial element of the Alt-Right, especially his claim that the neo-Nazis, who are such a vocal element of Alt-Right

Twitter, represent just a small element of the movement. Unsurprisingly, the most strident critics of Yiannopoulos and others in the Alt-Lite are found at the *Daily Stormer*, where Andrew Anglin declared, "I am hereby declaring a Holy Crusade against Milo Yiannopoulos, who is the single greatest threat our movement has at this time."[16] They are particularly incensed by Yiannopoulos's insistence that the Alt-Right is not really about race. Anglin also called for a complete Alt-Right boycott of *Breitbart* as long as it employed Yiannopoulos.[17] The *Daily Stormer* has denounced other figures associated with the Alt-Lite with similar ferocity, declaring that "Kike-Lover Lauren Southern Should Shut Her Slut Mouth" because "she's doing the Milo thing, going around saying she doesn't represent us but we aren't racists and blah blah blah."[18]

The writers at *The Right Stuff* did not go quite that far, but they were similarly concerned about Yiannopoulos and the degree to which he was becoming associated with the Alt-Right in the popular media. For that reason, a writer at the site sought to clarify the record, insisting that the similarities between Yiannopoulos' political philosophy and the Alt-Right are, at most, superficial:

> I'm writing this article to give what I think is a much needed reminder about what we want, and who Milo is. I'm not writing this because I want to cause drama. If Milo had remained on the periphery of our movement, pushing the Overton Window rightward, I'd be happy to ignore him. Unfortunately, both inside and outside of the Alt-Right there are people who are starting to consider him one of the principal leaders of the movement. *The Daily Beast* recently termed him the young face of the Alt-Right.

> It's time for a gentle reminder that Milo isn't one of us.[19]

Other voices on the Alt-Right have been more sanguine about the Alt-Lite phenomenon. A writer at *American Renaissance* argued that "the Alt-Lite has a place in our movement" because it can open people up to more radical ideas.[20] He went on to note that the "average 'normie' is more receptive to hearing these messages from Milo Yiannopoulos than from Jared Taylor, much less from @Pepe_Stormtrooper1488." Hunter Wallace suggested at *Occidental Dissent* that "every Alt-Lite moderate out there is a potential budding radical."[21] Richard Spencer also suggested that the Alt-Right can only benefit from the new attention the movement is receiving, even when it is being promoted by people outside the movement that do not share the Alt-Right's most basic premises—such as Yiannopoulos. When I asked him about this, he said:

> I was a little disappointed, although I understand their position, with people that were attacking Milo—because I do think that race should be an essential quality to the Alt-Right, unquestionably. I held a press conference where I said just that. However, I think we would be wrong not to recognize this major achievement: that our ideas, maybe in a more palatable, maybe in a little watered-down form, are becoming popular and considered cool by college kids. That's something that the [paleoconservatives] never had any hope of achieving. That's where we are now. . . . People that maybe formerly would have been fairly mainstream conservatives are breaking away from it . . . there are people who recognize them-

selves as conservative but want to do it with a totally new style, in a totally new key.[22]

I similarly asked Greg Johnson—who declared in 2016 that "The Alt-Right Means White Nationalism . . . or Nothing at All"[23]—what he thought about people who call themselves Alt-Right supporters but who also claim to reject racism. He said the following:

> The term "Alt Right" is a vague umbrella term that encompasses all people who reject mainstream conservatism. Now of course that includes many people who are not racially aware. So the Alt Right is White Nationalist not in the sense that all Alt Rightists are White Nationalists. Instead, the Alt Right is White Nationalist in the sense that the original *Alternative Right* webzine was founded as a vehicle by which White Nationalists could interact with dissident Rightists who were closer to the mainstream in order to convert them to our way of thinking. So the Alt Right consists of a hard inner core of White Nationalists and a flabby periphery of other edgy dissident Rightists who are happy to have a generic term, "Alt Right," that does not commit them to anything outside their comfort zone. The dynamic of the Alt Right has been to "red pill" and convert the best of these lurkers to a White Nationalist outlook. Those who are unconverted will either remain in our circle because they are comfortable being around White Nationalists and thus serve as bridges and lines of influence to the mainstream, or if they are uncomfortable with the presence of White Nationalists, they will leave. But we aren't

> leaving. We built this house, and we will burn it to the ground before we allow ourselves to be evicted from it.[24]

It is worth noting that, on the question of how the Alt-Right should be classified, the most racist elements of the Alt-Right agree with the Alt-Right's conservative opponents. Jonah Goldberg argued in *National Review*, for example, that no one should ever lose sight of the Alt-Right's racial angle or try to downplay its most racist elements.[25] Instead, according to Goldberg, everyone who adopts the Alt-Right label should know that they are throwing their lot in with white supremacists.

GROWING TENSIONS

In the months following the 2016 presidential election, tensions between the core of the Alt-Right and the peripheral Alt-Lite became more pronounced. Although some central Alt-Right voices had criticized Spencer for the Nazi salutes displayed at the postelection NPI conference, key Alt-Lite figures took this criticism a step further. Cernovich went so far as to say that Spencer was "controlled opposition" and perhaps even a government operative—though Cernovich subsequently backed down from this claim and removed the article where he made this accusation from his website.

The most dramatic schism between the Alt-Right and Trump's less radical right-wing supporters occurred in December during the organization of the "Deploraball"—a party celebrating Trump's victory, so named because of Hillary Clinton's earlier comments about Trump supporters being a "basket of deplorables." The event was predominantly spearheaded by Cernovich and included speakers such as McInnes. Most of the people involved with organizing the event, although definitely right wing, cannot be classified as Alt-Right. The one exception was a prolific Twitter user named Tim Treadstone, who went by the name "Baked Alaska." Treadstone found himself at odds with the other organizers when he wrote a tweet bringing up the issue of Jewish influence in the media[26]—a common white-nationalist talking point. Following a spat via Twitter direct messages (which were subsequently published online),[27] Treadstone was disinvited from the event. This led to a barrage of accusations that Cernovich was a "cuck," as was everyone else associated with the Deploraball.[28]

For his part, Cernovich argued that the controversy was actually useful in that it helped further distinguish his movement (and by extension, the overall Trump phenomenon) from the radicalism of the Alt-Right:

> We have a nice line of demarcation, so I'm happy with where I am and how it shook out. There's the alt-right which wants to do white identity politics, and then there's people like me and Jeff [Giesea] who, we want to do nationalism without white identity politics, and now everybody knows where I stand and everybody knows where everybody else is, so I'm thrilled with the development.[29]

Paul Joseph Watson similarly declared that there needed to be a clear line of separation between the racial aspect of the Alt-Right and others that have been associated with the movement but disavow white nationalism:

> There are two "Alt-Rights."
>
> One is more accurately described as the New Right. These people like to wear MAGA hats, create memes, & have fun.
>
> They include whites, blacks, Asians, latinos, gays and everyone else. These are the people who helped Trump win the election.
>
> The other faction likes to fester in dark corners of sub-reddits and obsess about Jews, racial superiority, and Adolf Hitler.
>
> This is a tiny fringe minority. They had no impact on the election.[30]

Mike Cernovich also endorsed the term "new right" to disaggregate his positions from those of the Alt-Right.[31] At the time of this writing, this term has not really caught on. It is questionable that it will ever be widely adopted, given the disparate movements that already use the label. The European New Right is one example. The mainstream conservative coalition that put Ronald Reagan in the White House similarly described itself as the "New Right" at the time.[32]

In early 2017, Yiannopoulos also sought to place a greater distance between himself and the Alt-Right, affirming his opposition to white-identity politics:

> The reality is, if you force everyone to play identity politics, if you insist in pitting whites against blacks, women against men, straights against gays, the reality is [whites] are gonna win and the left isn't going to like it very much. But there's a better way, you know? Don't fight identity politics with identity politics. White pride, white nationalism, white supremacy isn't the way to go.

> The way to go is reminding them and yourselves that you should be aspiring to values and to ideas. You should be focusing on what unites people and not what drives them apart. You shouldn't give a shit about skin color, a shit about sexuality. You shouldn't give a shit about gender, and you should be deeply suspicious of the people who do.[33]

Yiannopoulos's open break with the Alt-Right, which he once defended, seemed to be paying dividends. He secured a major book deal with a six-figure advance and was offered a major speaking slot at the 2017 CPAC (the Conservative Political Action Conference, the conservative movement's most important annual gathering). Shortly before CPAC, however, his career suffered a massive blow—though not because of any of his comments about immigration, Islam, or women. In February 2017, videos of Yiannopoulos defending pederasty and even glorifying the sexual abuse he suffered as a child surfaced.[34] Within days, Yiannopoulos's speech at CPAC was canceled, he lost his book deal, and he resigned from *Breitbart.*

Breitbart as a whole seems to be transitioning to a more mainstream media platform, if its recent hires are any indication. For example, Kristina Wong (formerly at *The Hill*), Sam Chi (formerly at *RealClearPolitics*), and John Carney (formerly at the *Wall Street Journal*) were all hired by *Breitbart* following Trump's election.[35] Given the current political climate, with Bannon a key figure in the Trump administration, it probably makes sense for *Breitbart* to back away from its pose as a venue for political dissidents. It similarly makes sense for *Breitbart* to end its flirtation with the Alt-Right and act like a powerful mainstream-media empire. But this also carries risks. As Callum Borchers noted in the *Washington Post*, "Yiannopoulos and Breitbart are, of course, free to capitalize on their support of Trump's successful campaign and to try to broaden their audience. But if they want to go mainstream, they risk alienating readers who were drawn to the website because it seemed to be by and for outsiders."[36]

Given these recent controversies and public statements, it appears that the white nationalists have won the battle for the Alt-Right label. Those who are not comfortable associating with white nationalism seem to be backing away from the term, making the Alt-Right a less ideologically diverse movement than it might have otherwise become. The question is whether this will ultimately prove to be a Pyrrhic victory for the Alt-Right. If the gap between the Alt-Right and these more mainstream figures becomes clearer, the end result may be that fewer people transition from being fans of *Breitbart* to fans of the *Daily Stormer* or *The Right Stuff*.

But it remains unclear how many people joined the more radical Alt-Right after consuming material from the Alt-Lite. As mentioned above, much of the Alt-Right hoped that these mainstream figures could act as an entry point to more extreme positions. As Lawrence Murray put it, "the Alt-Lite is our hunting ground."[37] Yet it is not obvious to me that the Alt-Lite pushed a substantial number of people into the Alt-Right. In none of my interviews did I encounter someone who said he or she was nudged into white nationalism by Yiannopoulos, Cernovich, or any of the other figures associated with the Alt-Lite. Robert Carter also noted this in an article at *The Right Stuff*: "Milo was even frequently discussed on the Alt Right as a potential gateway drug to more substantial identitarian attitudes. In reality there was never evidence of this—to my knowledge, no new arrival to an Alt Right conference or informal gathering ever identified Milo as a prime influence or motivator."[38] But the Alt-Lite did play a role in pushing the mainstream discussion on questions of race and immigration to the right, which is consequential even if it did not create a new crop of Alt-Right white nationalists.

CONCLUSION

Any political movement, if it grows large enough, will experience splits that lead to new debates about taxonomies. Within the far left in the twentieth century we saw the divide between Stalinists, Trotskyists, Maoists, and too many others to name here. Libertarians remain divided between anarchists, minarchists, and "low-tax liberals." Aside from the paleoconservative-neoconservative divide, mainstream conservatives have been divided on multiple questions since the movement's inception (on Burkeanism, for example). The Alt-Right is no different, but there is a yawning gap between the "cultural libertarians" complaining about oppressive political correctness and the neo-Nazis on /pol/. Even the big tent that is the Alt-Right may be too small to contain these different sensibilities.

CONCLUSION

There are several important questions we cannot yet answer definitively. Is the Alt-Right really here to stay, or was it a short-term phenomenon, representing just one of the many ways the 2016 presidential election cycle was unique? And if the Alt-Right is not going away, is it going to grow? Will it remain a purely online movement? If not, what will it look like when it moves into the real world? Finally, if the Alt-Right is not going to go away on its own and has the potential for growth, how can it be managed or weakened?

Everything we have seen over the past year suggests that the Alt-Right will stick around for the foreseeable future. Donald Trump's victory emboldened the Alt-Right like never before, and it will do everything it can to capitalize on its momentum. In the long term, Hillary Clinton's decision to bring the Alt-Right into the national conversation may have been a strategic mistake from the progressive perspective. Although I maintain that the connection between Trump and the Alt-Right is tenuous, by forcefully declaring such a connection, Clinton raised the stakes of the 2016 election by implying that a Trump victory represented an Alt-Right victory. At the time, this made some sense. Most Americans probably would be turned off by the most aggressive rhetoric of the Alt-Right. But once that connection was made, with Trump's win in the Electoral College (though not the popular vote), the Alt-Right could reasonably claim to share Trump's victory. The Twitter account associated with VDare.com made this point immediately after Clinton made her address about the Alt-Right, stating: "Interesting side effect—media and #Crooked-Hillary have really put themselves out there. If this doesn't work, #AltRight can't be suppressed."[1]

Among the Alt-Right's opponents, there is not a consensus regarding how to deal with the movement. One option has been put forth by those who are sympathetic to certain elements of the Alt-Right: give the Alt-Right at least some of what it demands. Milo Yiannopoulos made this argument in a speech titled "How to Destroy the Alt-Right."[2] He argued that if political correctness is reined in, if people with dissident views are given a fair hearing, if mass immigration is brought to a halt, and if different groups cease to be held to different standards regarding acceptable behavior, then much of the anger that fuels the Alt-Right will dissipate. He argued that the left either has to abandon identity politics entirely or make peace with a permanent constituency for white-identity politics.

To the Alt-Right's primary opponents, this hardly counts as a solution at all. Yes, capitulating to the Alt-Right on most of its demands, stopping short of white nationalism, will probably cost the Alt-Right some of its support. But even if there was a widespread agreement that American society should make a sharp turn to the right in order to assuage the Alt-Right, this would surely not lead to a new era of social peace. For instance, one of Yiannopoulos's suggestions for achieving this Alt-Right appeasement was to "criminalize

Black Lives Matter."[3] This is not going to be implemented or even endorsed by mainstream conservatives.

Furthermore, it is naïve to expect that the Alt-Right will be content to declare victory and go home just because two-thirds of its agenda has been implemented. If the direction of American politics starts moving to the right, it is a good bet that agitators will continue to push it further in that direction.

Some commentators have suggested that the Alt-Right must not be placated at all. They want it to be clear that the mainstream conservative movement represents the dividing line between acceptable and unacceptable opinion—those to the right of that line are to be shunned and ostracized. If such a narrative took hold, it might slow the growth of the Alt-Right and perhaps shrink it further. But this strategy also carries risks. By forcing additional polarization, telling Americans with right-wing inclinations that they must choose between the *Weekly Standard* and neo-Nazi discussion boards, with no acceptable middle ground on the right, conservatives may draw some people away from the Alt-Right, especially those who are on the periphery of the movement. But with mainstream conservatism at a low point of credibility, such a move may push others farther to the political right. By declaring that every American to the right of David Brooks is a deplorable Nazi, conservatives may inadvertently play into the hands of the Alt-Right's most radical extremists—just as insisting that every Muslim is a potential terrorist or terrorist supporter may aid the growth of groups like ISIS.

Some have suggested that the Alt-Right can be dealt a crippling blow if there is more vigorous policing of the Internet—and much of the Alt-Right apparently agrees that this would be devastating to the movement. Social media, especially Twitter, has been the primary means by which the Alt-Right penetrates public discourse. Its ability to do so in the future is contingent on social media remaining generally free from meaningful censorship. If Twitter and related sites cease to be an online Wild West and if the owners of these sites begin to police user activity aggressively, shutting down racist commentary, the Alt-Right will be back in its Internet isolation.

At the time of this writing, there is some evidence that greater censorship of Twitter will be forthcoming. In early 2016, Twitter announced the creation of a "Trust and Safety Council."[4] The announcement assured readers that Twitter remains committed to free speech, but it also said it would work with experts to "prevent abuse, harassment, and bullying." Voices on the Alt-Right were particularly concerned to see the Anti-Defamation League included in this council, as this seemed to signal that Twitter was going to start censoring racist and anti-Semitic posts.

Also in early 2016, Twitter began to take action against certain figures on the right. Curiously, the Alt-Right did not seem to be an early target. To my knowledge, the first notable person on the right to face a Twitter ban was Robert Stacy McCain[5]—a fairly conventional conservative. Although McCain was a strong critic of feminism, his writings were not uniquely inflammatory or really that far outside the conservative norm. Twitter also took action against Yiannopoulos by removing his "verified" status.[6] He was later banned from the platform entirely after some of his remarks prompted a deluge of hateful comments aimed at the actress Leslie Jones.[7] Twitter also banned a Twitter user named Ricky Vaughn, who was not just the most influential Alt-Right voice on Twitter but one of the most influential Twitter personalities from anywhere on the ideological spectrum, according to one study conducted by MIT.[8]

There are also rumors that Twitter has begun to "shadow ban" certain users—blocking a user's tweets from automatically showing up in his or her follower's feeds without taking any formal action. Twitter took even more dramatic steps following the election results, suspending the accounts of multiple prominent Alt-Right figures, including Pax Dickinson, John Rivers, Paul Town, and Richard Spencer.[9] In a short video released shortly after these bans occurred, Spencer described Twitter's decision as act of "corporate Stalinism, in the sense that there is a great purge going on, and they're purging people on the basis of their views."[10] Once again, Twitter's choices regarding which accounts to suspend, permanently or otherwise, seemed somewhat arbitrary. Rivers's comments on Twitter likely violated the platform's hate-speech policies, but Spencer was more careful in his choice of language on social media. And many of the more radical and offensive Alt-Right Twitter accounts were untouched by this purge.

Unless there is total government control of the Internet, radical political views will always be present online. However, censorship at places like Twitter has the potential to create real problems for the Alt-Right and other radical online movements. The Alt-Right was able to inject itself into the conversation by entering spaces predominantly occupied by people outside the movement. If they are denied access to these spaces, the far right may find itself back where it was when white nationalists congregated at places like Stormfront, where they engaged with one another but otherwise could be ignored. The Alt-Right could presumably create its own social-network sites (in fact, the new social-media site Gab seems to have been created for this purpose),[11] but it is difficult to see what this would accomplish if they fail to attract people outside the movement—they would just end up trolling one another.

Yet even some of the Alt-Right's most vocal opponents have criticized Twitter for banning Alt-Right accounts. David Frum, who is a frequent target of Alt-Right insults, suggested denying people a platform to speak simply because they have offensive opinions would only strengthen the Alt-Right's narrative about censorship: "It's precisely the perception of arbitrary and one-sided speech policing that drives so many young men toward radical, illiberal politics. On campus especially, but also in the corporate world—and now on social media—they perceive that wild and wacky things can be said by some people, but not by others."[12] Frum went on to suggest that the best way to combat the Alt-Right is to have reasonable debates about the important topics they want to discuss, while still forcefully rejecting the Alt-Right's vision:

> Over the past two decades, Americans have constructed systems of intellectual silencing that stifle the range of debate among responsible and public-spirited people. They've resigned hugely important topics to the domain of cranks and haters. If the only people who'll talk about the risks and costs of a more diverse society are fascists, then the fascists will gain an audience. So long as they refrain from incitement and harassment, the right way to deal with social media's neo-Nazis is not by taking away their platforms, but by taking away their audiences, by welcoming a more open and more intelligent discussion of what Americans yearn most to hear about.[13]

The future of the Alt-Right on Twitter became even less clear when, weeks after his ban from the platform, Spencer's account was reinstated—though the account for the website

Radix remained blocked. Thus, at the time of this writing, the Alt-Right does not appear to be in immediate danger of being shut out of Twitter. But the platform's capricious attitude toward the Alt-Right (and radical speech in general) suggests that it may, at some point in the future, crack down on the movement.

Besides facing a questionable future on Twitter, the Alt-Right suffered a significant loss when Reddit shut down the popular subreddit known as "r/altright," purportedly because its users were engaging in doxing.[14] Reddit has a deserved reputation as a hub for free speech on the Internet, and it rarely bans communities, so this move was significant.

Even if the Alt-Right finds itself blocked from Twitter and similar sites, the movement has previously found ways to work around efforts to stamp out offensive speech online. For example, in order to get around bans on racial slurs, the Alt-Right has begun to use the names of major corporate entities as code words for minority groups. For example, some on the Alt-Right have begun referring to African Americans as "googles" and Jews as "skypes"—terms that obviously cannot be banned from the Internet. When major online platforms try to block one medium for spreading Alt-Right propaganda, the army of online trolls immediately looks for weaknesses in the armor, and it usually finds one.

Increasing online censorship in order to weaken the Alt-Right creates an additional problem. The Internet is an ideologically neutral tool. The entire political spectrum uses it to organize and spread messages. In the long run, progressives may want to be cautious about calling for greater government and corporate control over the major Internet platforms. Rules used against the Alt-Right today can be used against Occupy Wall Street or Black Lives Matter tomorrow.

There is one final problem with efforts to block the Alt-Right from major online venues: it may be too late. The movement may have already achieved escape velocity. During the week that Spencer was banned from Twitter, he was also a pervasive presence in the media, covered in multiple newspapers and even interviewed on National Public Radio—hardly a forum known for giving racists a platform. The organizers of the 2017 CPAC were sufficiently alarmed by the Alt-Right to dedicate a speech entirely to the subject, warning attendees that the Alt-Right "is a sinister organization that is trying to worm its way in, into our ranks."[15] Too many people are now aware of the Alt-Right for the movement to be quietly suppressed and forgotten.

Members of the Alt-Right are annoyed when they face roadblocks from their preferred venues for spreading their message, but these challenges do not at this point pose the movement any kind of existential threat. However, opponents of the movement have recently embraced doxing as a more aggressive means of opposing the Alt-Right. This method of attack is much more dramatic, given the consequences for the people involved. The number of people who openly and publicly support the Alt-Right is dwarfed by the number of people who privately support the movement. Those who wish to get involved without facing serious repercussions in their personal lives typically do so by creating pennames, creating anonymous Twitter accounts, and posting anonymously to various message boards. But simply using a penname is not a guarantee of long-term anonymity, especially if a person on the Alt-Right is not careful about leaving clues about his or her real identity. In late 2016 and early 2017, the Alt-Right faced its most dramatic doxing cases to date.

The first major Alt-Right personality to suffer doxing during this period was a Scottish video blogger who used the name "Millennial Woes." Although he never revealed his name in any of his videos, he did not mask his voice or hide his face. As he grew in popularity (his YouTube channel had millions of views), it was probably inevitable that his real identity would be revealed—and in January 2017 it was made public by the press in the United Kingdom.[16]

Shortly after Millennial Woes's doxing, the Alt-Right suffered a more significant setback: the doxing of key figures associated with *The Right Stuff*,[17] including Mike Enoch, whose doxing included the revelation that his wife was Jewish.[18] *TRS* immediately came under heavy fire from other corners of the Alt-Right, including some previously affiliated with *TRS*—at least two podcasts hosted by *TRS* cut ties with the site in the following days. Some opponents of the Alt-Right quickly declared that *TRS* was finished. *Salon*, for example, declared that Enoch had resigned from his own platform as a result of the scandal, which was not actually true.[19]

As it turned out, although these doxing incidents were no doubt disastrous for the people who were exposed (Enoch lost both his job and his marriage), they had little impact on their subsequent content creation. Millennial Woes, Mike Enoch, and many of the other people exposed by these doxing efforts continued to produce videos and podcasts. And Enoch was not universally shunned; Richard Spencer, for example, announced his support for Enoch on Twitter,[20] and Greg Johnson wrote a long essay defending Enoch from his critics on the far right.[21] Perhaps most surprising, Enoch even received support from the *Daily Stormer*'s Andrew Anglin, who argued that Enoch's personal life did not diminish his contribution to the movement. Anglin additionally argued against massive hostility toward Enoch because "What the Jews want is for us to eat ourselves."[22] Given this, one could argue that doxing is counterproductive, since doxing victims will have no disincentive to stop creating Alt-Right content after being revealed. Indeed, they may become even more energetic and well known, as they no longer need to hide their identities.

But while doxing is not necessarily a useful means of silencing one particular voice, it may have greater unseen effects: it sends a message to others, encouraging them to stop their work in the Alt-Right or dissuading them from getting involved in the first place. For example, the most consequential outcome of the doxing at *TRS* was the end of the popular *Fash the Nation* podcast; the hosts of that program, even though they had not been exposed, quickly deleted their website following the *TRS* doxing.

An increased threat of doxing presents a real problem for the Alt-Right. At the front of the movement, there are figures who openly use their real names and show their faces in public (Spencer, Anglin, Nathan Damigo, etc.). On the other end of the spectrum, there are thousands of truly anonymous Internet users posting on social media and on message boards. But there are also many who fall somewhere in the middle, writing consistently under the same penname, appearing on podcasts using their real voices, or showing up at Alt-Right events. These are people who have something to lose and who do not want their real lives intertwined with their political activities. But by being anything other than totally anonymous online trolls, these activists risk leaving clues about their identity. The danger of doxing may dissuade many Alt-Right supporters from entering into that middle category—a category that includes many of the movement's most energetic figures. An

Alt-Right Twitter user writing under the name Joshua Graham agreed that a clear bifurcation within the movement is probably the way forward for the Alt-Right: "One should either remain totally anon or just proudly not give a fuck and be themselves."[23]

In recent weeks, the Alt-Right's opponents have increasingly turned to a more dramatic strategy: real-world confrontations, sometimes violent. In 2016, there was a clash between Matthew Heimbach's Traditionalist Workers Party and antiracist protesters in Sacramento, for example.[24] And in Washington, D.C., on the day of President Trump's inauguration, while having a conversation with journalists, Richard Spencer was surprised and assaulted by a masked attacker, who subsequently vanished into a crowd and has not, at the time of this writing, been identified.[25] The entire episode was caught on camera and shared thousands of times on social media—predominantly by Spencer's critics.

In the weeks that followed, violence erupted at events involving other figures sometimes associated with the Alt-Right. When Milo Yiannopoulos attempted to give a speech at the University of California at Berkeley, protests quickly devolved into a violent riot, causing considerable damage to property and forcing the event's cancellation.[26] A similar, though less dramatic, confrontation occurred when Gavin McInnes was pepper sprayed at New York University before a planned speech that was subsequently cancelled.[27]

Of all the methods used against the Alt-Right, violent confrontation is the least likely to succeed in the long run. In all of the aforementioned cases, the targeted figures were engaging in constitutionally protected free speech—not in violence or in calling others to violence. One does not need to be an Alt-Right supporter to question whether combating illiberal viewpoints should or can be accomplished by rejecting the basic liberal value of free expression. And even if one does believe that the Alt-Right and peripheral movements are so dangerous that they should be violently suppressed, such tactics are unlikely to have their intended outcome. Part of the Alt-Right's core message is that white people are a persecuted group in society and that white advocates are especially likely to be victimized by progressives. When an Alt-Right figure is assaulted merely for expressing a viewpoint, such a narrative is only reinforced.

A greater danger is that antifascist attacks on the Alt-Right will provoke a counterresponse. As I stated in the introduction, the Alt-Right at present cannot be classified as a violent movement. It is possible that this will change in the future, and one thing likely to promote such a transition is a justifiable belief that supporters of the Alt-Right are in legitimate physical danger. At least some leading figures of the Alt-Right now intend to increase their security when in public. According to Richard Spencer shortly after his own attack, "We're going to need some better security. . . . I think we're going to start to need bodyguards."[28]

Some on the Alt-Right seem to welcome an excuse for the Alt-Right to transition from a mob of anonymous keyboard warriors to street fighters. As Matt Parrot put it in an article titled "I'm Glad Richard Spencer Got Punched in the Face":

> It's pretty unwise for the Left to be normalizing political violence given the way the wind's blowing. It doesn't take a genius to see that ours is the side with most of the guns, most of the veterans, most of the people who work out, and most of the people who can both execute and absorb a good solid punch. Our side avoids violence be-

> cause we're attempting to win a moral case. Our side avoids violence because the system's itching for any excuse to crack down on us. Our side avoids violence for a lot of reasons, but fear of losing a fight isn't one of them.[29]

Beyond outside efforts to combat the movement, legal or otherwise, the Alt-Right faces other challenges. As is the case in many political movements, there are important divisions within the Alt-Right's ranks, which may hinder future cooperation and effectiveness. A few minutes of browsing Alt-Right message boards are all it takes to appreciate the tremendous infighting within the movement. Different factions are incessantly accusing the others of being "shills" or "controlled opposition."

The white-nationalist movement in the United States has historically suffered from a persistent problem: various chiefs with small followings have been at the throats of their (equally marginalized) competitors. The amorphous nature of the Alt-Right today has somewhat mitigated this problem. As the movement lacks significant formal institutions, influential people on the Alt-Right are not fighting one another for members and donors. When two people on the Alt-Right have irreconcilable differences of opinion or temperament, they can simply avoid each other. Getting blocked from one Alt-Right website or forum does not preclude someone from creating new content elsewhere.

That said, divides in the movement are significant. Some of the disputes on the Alt-Right deal with important subjects. Besides the question of the Alt-Lite, the Alt-Right remains divided on issues of religion, on tolerance for homosexuals, on anti-Semitism, and, in the long run, whether the Alt-Right's ultimate goal is the creation of independent white ethnostates in Europe and North America or is instead the birth of a pan-European empire. These can all be papered over as long as the Alt-Right remains a loose movement, but for the movement to grow in the long term, they will need to be eventually resolved. This may not be possible.

In order to enjoy more significant success in the real world, the Alt-Right will need to start building actual institutions. Should that happen—for example, should we see ground break on the Alt-Right equivalent of the Heritage Foundation in the Beltway (something that strikes me as very implausible at the moment)—the movement will need to demonstrate greater cooperation and congeniality within its ranks than I have seen thus far. To grow, the Alt-Right may eventually need its own William F. Buckley: a universally revered figure in the movement whose declarations carry tremendous weight. At this point, I do not know who could fulfill such a role. The most well-known figures in the Alt-Right (Richard Spencer, Andrew Anglin, etc.) all have a long list of implacable critics within the movement's own ranks.

To move beyond being a nuisance on social media and actually to change the politics and culture of the United States, the Alt-Right will require a level of seriousness and organization it has not yet displayed. Although the Alt-Right needs to be taken seriously, anonymous Twitter accounts are not going to change the world fundamentally, especially if efforts to combat the Alt-Right continue to escalate. As Millennial Woes put it in a 2017 speech in Stockholm, Sweden:

> We know that in order to make further progress, we're going to have to get better in the Alt-Right. More organized, more methodical, more efficient, and in some

> ways more serious, more dedicated. And I learned that myself, recently. It's not a game anymore. It's not just a bedroom project anymore. And I think that goes not just for me but for everyone. . . . With all this string of doxings we've realized what's at stake. It is serious. And I think this idea of having to change kind of scares us. Because it's new and because it means discipline. And as I say it means the Alt-Right won't just be fun anymore.[30]

There are signs that higher levels of cooperation and organization within the Alt-Right are forthcoming. Significantly, in early 2017, Richard Spencer launched a new website intended to serve as the most significant platform of the Alt-Right to date: AltRight.com. The site combined the efforts of many already existing Alt-Right projects, including Arktos (the primary English-language source for European New Right material) and Red Ice (perhaps the most professional of all the Alt-Right online video and radio networks). The site also promised a forum that would take the place of the one shut down by Reddit—at the time of this writing, this forum had not been activated, though I have no reason to believe it will not be online by the time these words are published. Spencer also rented space in Alexandria, Va., to serve as a real-world presence for the Alt-Right.[31] We should not overstate the significance of this, as even some of the most insignificant conservative think tanks occupy more extravagant offices, but it is a first step toward taking the Alt-Right off of the Internet.

Although I think it is unlikely that the Alt-Right will fade into obscurity, the Alt-Right will also be judged as a failed movement if it continues to exist long into the future. By that I mean the Alt-Right presents itself as an *alternative* to the conservative movement. The existence of an Alt-Right depends on the existence of a mainstream to rebel against. What the Alt-Right ultimately wants is to drop the "Alt" from its name and instead become the new mainstream right. Until that happens, the Alt-Right is a nuisance, but one that lacks any substantive control over policy.

The most important question is whether this is a likely scenario. Although Trump's victory brought the Alt-Right to the nation's attention, and Trump's statements on immigration are broadly congruent with the Alt-Right's message, the Alt-Right still has no actual power. Trump's brand of populist nationalism is a major break from traditional conservatism, but it is a far cry from the explicit white nationalism and anti-Semitism of the Alt-Right. That said, it is too early to say whether the nation's rightward drift at the end of the 2016 will stop with Trump. Because the organized conservative movement, which has long been the primary policeman of the right, suffered a devastating blow when Trump defeated his conservative primary opponents, space has been opened up for more radical alternatives.

We do not yet know what direction the American right will take over the course of the Trump administration. It does appear, however, that the charge of racism seems to be losing its sting. Throughout the campaign, Trump (and by extension, anyone who supported Trump) was accused of racism. These allegations came mostly from the political left and center, but many conservatives similarly voiced this charge. It is telling that a majority of white Americans were willing to disregard this claim and vote for Trump anyway. I do not believe this signifies that a huge swath of white America secretly harbors Alt-Right beliefs. But we can be reasonably concerned that a growing percentage of white America no longer views racism as a moral failing and is willing to be associated with explicit white-identity politics. Whether traditional conservatives were sincere in their antiracism is beside the point. Conservatives at least paid lip service to the ideal of color-blind politics and denounced and purged open racists from their ranks. In a postconservative America, zero-sum identity politics may become the norm, and the Alt-Right will be on the periphery, pushing racial polarization at every available opportunity.

NOTES

INTRODUCTION

1. Nate Silver, "Here's How We're Forecasting the Four-Way Presidential Race in Utah," *FiveThirtyEight*, October 17, 2016, http://fivethirtyeight.com/features/heres-how-were-forecasting-the-4-way-presidential-race-in-utah/.
2. "Q&A with Matt Furie," *Know Your Meme*, January 25, 2011, http://knowyourmeme.com/blog/interviews/qa-with-matt-furie.
3. Sean T. Collins, "The Creator of Pepe the Frog Talks About Making Comics in the Post-Meme World," *Vice*, July 28, 2015, http://www.vice.com/read/feels-good-man-728.
4. Elizabeth Chan, "Donald Trump, Pepe the Frog, and White Supremacists: An Explainer," HillaryClinton.com, September 12, 2016, https://www.hillaryclinton.com/feed/donald-trump-pepe-the-frog-and-white-supremacists-an-explainer/.
5. RamZPaul, Twitter post, June 3, 2016, 5:16 p.m., https://twitter.com/ramzpaul/status/738887326550499330.
6. In chapter 5, I will discuss the Associated Press's guidelines regarding the Alt-Right.
7. Hunter Wallace, "What Is the Alt-Right?" *Occidental Dissent*, August 25, 2016, http://www.occidentaldissent.com/2016/08/25/what-is-the-alt-right/.
8. Specifically, I said: "Many on the left have long awaited the demise of conservatism as a force in America, and will cheer its

departure from the scene—should such a departure ever occur. However, progressives who seek the downfall of the conservative movement should be cautious in this regard. They are not the only ideologues who desperately wish to see American conservatism sent to the dustbin of history. . . . There are multiple right-wing movements that have been denied access to the mainstream political debate—largely due to the conservative movement's aggressive enforcement of the boundaries of acceptable right-wing thought. It is possible that a rapid implosion of mainstream conservatism will usher in a new progressive consensus in American politics. It is also possible that such an implosion will offer crucial breathing space for one or more of these alternative right-wing ideologies. In a post-conservative America, one or more of the ideologies discussed in this volume may find new followers and gain new wealthy benefactors who previously backed the mainstream conservative movement. While progressives may view some of these alternatives as superior to traditional conservatism—or at least not any worse—they will surely also view others as *much* more dangerous and threatening to their values. If conservatism breaks down, many of its present constituents may embrace a more radical right-wing ideology, making American politics far more unstable." George Hawley, *Right-Wing Critics of American Conservatism* (Lawrence: University Press of Kansas, 2016), 288.

9. Southern Poverty Law Center, "Alternative Right," https://www.splcenter.org/fighting-hate/extremist-files/ideology/alternative-right.
10. Benjamin Welton, "What, Exactly, is the 'Alternative Right'?" *Weekly Standard*, December 21, 2016, http://www.weeklystandard.com/what-exactly-is-the-alternative-right/article/2000310; Sarah Rathod, "How the So-Called 'Alt-Right' Went From the Fringe to the White House," *Mother Jones*, November 22, 2016, http://www.motherjones.com/politics/2016/11/alt-right-timeline-bannon-breitbart-trump.

1. THE ALT-RIGHT'S GOALS AND PREDECESSORS

1. Brendan O'Connor, "Here Is What Appears to Be Dylann Roof's Racist Manifesto," *Gawker*, June 20, 2015, http://gawker.com/here-is-what-appears-to-be-dylann-roofs-racist-manifest-1712767241. Harold Covington has been involved with various white-nationalist organizations in the United States for decades. In recent years, he has been pushing for all white nationalists in North America to move to the Pacific Northwest and make plans to secede from the United States to create a new, all-white nation. He has written four novels that describe a future war for independence in the Northwest.
2. To take just one ominous example of what may be coming: the lawyers for a man who threatened to kill Muslims in America claimed that he had been radicalized by the Alt-Right. Christopher Mathias, "Lawyers Blame Alt-Right for Client's Death Threats Against Muslims," *Huffington Post*, November 5, 2016, http://www.huffingtonpost.com/entry/lawyers-blame-alt-right-for-clients-death-threats-against-muslims_us_581c9e9be4b0e80b02c93e24.
3. Yggdrasil, "What Is White Nationalism?" http://www.whitenationalism.com/wn/wn-06.htm.
4. Benjamin Garland, "Jew Admits to Dreams of Defiling Aryan Blood," *Daily Stormer*, May 26, 2016, http://www.dailystormer.com/taylorswiftwasright-jew-admits-to-dreams-of-defiling-aryan-blood/.
5. Colin Liddell, "Joining the Dots on Andrew Anglin," *Alternative Right*, September 1, 2016, http://alternative-right.blogspot.com/2016/09/joining-dots-on-andrew-anglin.html.
6. RamZPaul, "Punching (((Right))): Wrangling with Anglin," *Alternative Right*, December 9, 2016, http://alternative-right.blogspot.com/2016/12/punching-right-wrangling-with-anglin.html/.
7. Personal interview with Richard Spencer, October 12, 2016.
8. Ibid.
9. Greg Johnson, "To Cleanse America: Some Practical Solutions," *Counter-Currents* October 27, 2010, http://www.counter-currents.com/2010/10/to-cleanse-america/.

10. Ibid.
11. Uriah, Twitter post, November 23, 2016, 6:56 p.m., https://twitter.com/crimkadid/status/801620520273932288.
12. "How to Set Up an Alt-Right Meet Up in Your Area," *Amerika*, October 31, 2016, http://www.amerika.org/politics/how-to-set-up-an-alt-right-meetup-in-your-area/.
13. Thomas Jefferson, "Notes on the State of Virginia, Queries 14 and 18, 137–43, 162–63 [1784]," *The Founder's Constitution*, http://press-pubs.uchicago.edu/founders/documents/v1ch15s28.html.
14. Christa Dierksheide "'The Great Improvement and Civilization of that Race': Jefferson and the 'Amelioration' of Slavery, ca. 1770–1826," *Early American Studies: An Interdisciplinary Journal* 6 (2008): 165–197.
15. Jared Taylor, "What the Founding Fathers Really Thought About Race," National Policy Institute, January 17, 2012, http://www.npiamerica.org/research/category/what-the-founders-really-thought-about-race.
16. Caitlin Cruz, "Sanders Tells Liberty U: Sorry, but the U.S. Was Founded on 'Racist Principles,'" *TalkingPointsMemo*, September 14, 2015, http://talkingpointsmemo.com/livewire/bernie-sanders-liberty-university-racism-bible-verses.
17. Anti-Defamation League, "Tattered Robes: The State of the Ku Klux Klan in the United States," May 11, 2016, http://www.adl.org/combating-hate/domestic-extremism-terrorism/c/tattered-robes-the-state-of-the-kkk-in-the-us.html.
18. Louis Nelson, "Clinton Ad Ties Trump to KKK, White Supremacists," *Politico*, August 25, 2016, http://www.politico.com/story/2016/08/clinton-ad-kkk-trump-227404.
19. Meow Blitz, "Families of Holocaust Survivors and Victims Share Their Stories at Chapman," *The Right Stuff*, May 22, 2015, http://therightstuff.biz/2015/05/22/families-of-holocaust-survivors-share-their-stories-at-chapman/.
20. Southern Poverty Law Center, "American Renaissance," https://www.splcenter.org/fighting-hate/extremist-files/group/american-renaissance.
21. Jared Taylor, *Paved with Good Intentions: The Failure of Race Relations in Contemporary America* (New York: Carol and Graf, 1992).

22. Southern Poverty Law Center, "Jared Taylor," https://www.splcenter.org/fighting-hate/extremist-files/individual/jared-taylor.
23. Kevin MacDonald, *A People That Shall Dwell Alone: Judaism as a Group Evolutionary Strategy, with Diaspora Peoples* (Westport, Conn.: Praeger, 1994); Kevin MacDonald, *Separation and Its Discontents: Toward an Evolutionary Theory of Anti-Semitism* (Westport, Conn.: Praeger, 1998); Kevin MacDonald, *The Culture of Critique: An Evolutionary Analysis of Jewish Involvement in Twentieth-Century Intellectual and Political Movements* (Westport, Conn.: Praeger, 1998).
24. While working on this project, I asked Johnson a few questions about himself and the Alt-Right. Rather than respond to me directly, he answered these questions on his own website: Greg Johnson, "Interview on White Nationalism and the Alt-Right," *Counter-Currents*, October 19, 2016, http://www.counter-currents.com/2016/10/interview-on-white-nationalism-and-the-alt-right/.
25. For a lengthy discussion of the European New Right, see George Hawley, *Right-Wing Critics of American Conservatism* (Lawrence: University Press of Kansas, 2016), 207–242; Tamir Bar-On, *Rethinking the French New Right: Alternatives to Modernity* (New York: Routledge, 2013); Tamir Bar-On, *Where Have All the Fascists Gone?* (Burlington, Vt.: Ashgate, 2007).
26. Greg Johnson, "Frequently Asked Questions Part 1," *Counter-Currents*, June 5, 2012, http://www.counter-currents.com/2012/06/frequently-asked-questions-part-1/.
27. Joseph Scotchie, *The Paleoconservatives: New Voices for the Old Right* (New Brunswick, N.J.: Transaction, 1999), 1.
28. Christ Woltermann, "What Is Paleoconservatism?" *Telos* 97 (1993): 9.
29. M. E. Bradford, "On Remembering Who We Are: A Political Credo," *Modern Age* 26 (1982): 149.
30. Mark Gerson, *The Neoconservative Vision: From the Cold War Years to the Culture Wars* (New York: Madison, 1996), 315.
31. Patrick Buchanan, *Suicide of a Superpower: Will America Survive Until 2025?* (New York: St. Martin's Press, 2011), 123.

32. For an influential example of this argument, see Milton Friedman, *Capitalism and Freedom*, 40th anniversary ed. (Chicago: University of Chicago Press, 2002), 108–118.
33. Murray Rothbard defined the nonaggression principle this way: "The libertarian creed rests upon one central axiom: that no man or group of men may aggress against the person or property of anyone else. This may be called the 'nonaggression axiom.' 'Aggression' is defined as the initiation of the use or threat of physical violence against the person or property of anyone else." Murray Rothbard, *For a New Liberty* (1973; repr., Auburn, Ala.: Ludwig von Mises Institute, 2006), 27.
34. Murray Rothbard, "Egalitarianism as a Revolt Against Nature," *Modern Age* (December 1973): 350.
35. Murray Rothbard, *The Irrepressible Rothbard* (Burlington: Center for Libertarian Studies, 2000), 391.
36. Hans-Hermann Hoppe, *Democracy: The God That Failed* (New Brunswick, N.J.: Transaction, 2001).
37. Hans-Hermann Hoppe, "On Free Immigration and Forced Integration," LewRockwell.com, https://www.lewrockwell.com/1970/01/hans-hermann-hoppe/on-free-immigration-and-forced-integration/.
38. Llewellyn H. Rockwell Jr., "Open Borders: A Libertarian Reappraisal," LewRockwell.com, November 10, 2015, https://www.lewrockwell.com/2015/11/lew-rockwell/open-borders-assault-private-property/.
39. Richard Spencer, "The End of Rand Paul . . . and Libertarian Populism," *Radix*, February 4, 2016, http://www.radixjournal.com/blog/2016/2/4/the-end-of-rand-paul-and-libertarian-populism.
40. Conor Lynch, "Libertarianism Is for White Men: The Ugly Truth About the Right's Favorite Movement," *Salon*, June 10, 2015, http://www.salon.com/2015/06/10/why_libertarianism_is_so_popular_on_the_right_its_the_last_bastion_of_white_male_dominance/.
41. To get a sense of the arguments made by the original opponents of modern political thinking, I recommend Christopher Olaf

Bloom, *Critics of the Enlightenment* (Wilmington, De.: ISI, 2004).

42. Alain de Benoist, *On Being a Pagan* (Atlanta, Ga.: Ultra, 2004).
43. "Meet the IB, Europe's Version of America's Alt-Right," *Economist*, November 12, 2016, http://www.economist.com/news/europe/21709986-france-austria-identitarian-movement-gives-xenophobia-youthful-edge-meet-ib.
44. Robert L. Bartley, "Open NAFTA Borders? Why Not?" *Wall Street Journal*, July 2, 2001, http://www.wsj.com/articles/SB994028904620983237 .
45. "McCain Stands Alone on Immigration Bill," CNN, June 6, 2007, http://www.cnn.com/2007/POLITICS/06/05/debate.immigration/index.html.
46. Peter Brimelow, *Alien Nation: Common Sense About America's Immigration Disaster* (New York: Random House, 1995).
47. For example, see "Rethinking Immigration," *National Review*, August 17, 2007, http://www.nationalreview.com/article/221873/rethinking-immigration-editors.
48. Specifically, Brimelow told me the following: "VDARE.com is a forum site. We publish anyone critical of the post-1965 Immigration Disaster. We even publish Democrats! Immigration is a key issue for the Alt Right—as distinct from the Buckleyite 'American Conservative Movement'—and I would regard some of our younger writers e.g. James Kirkpatrick as Alt Rightists." E-mail interview with Peter Brimelow, January 11, 2017.
49. Mark Steyn, *America Alone: The End of the World as We Know It* (Washington, D.C.: Regnery, 2006); Glenn Beck, *It IS About Islam: Exposing the Truth About ISIS, Al Qaeda, Iran, and the Caliphate* (New York: Threshold, 2015); Pamela Geller, *Stop the Islamization of America: A Practical Guide to the Resistance* (New York: WND, 2011); Robert Spencer, *The Truth About Muhammad: Founder of the World's Most Intolerant Religion* (Washington, D.C.: Regnery, 2006).
50. Mark Steyn, "The Morning After," *SteynOnline*, February 15, 2016, http://www.steynonline.com/6813/the-morning-after.

51. Sean Illing, "Donald Trump and the Tea Party Myth: Why the GOP Is Now an Identity Movement, Not a Political Party," *Salon*, August 5, 2016, http://www.salon.com/2016/08/05/donald-trump-and-the-tea-party-myth-why-the-gop-is-now-an-identity-movement-not-a-political-party/.
52. For just a few recent examples of these, see Kim R. Holmes, *The Closing of the Liberal Mind: How Groupthink and Intolerance Define the Left* (New York: Encounter, 2016); Kimberley Strassel, *The Intimidation Game: How the Left Is Silencing Free Speech* (New York: Twelve, 2016); Mary Katherine Ham and Guy Benson, *End of Discussion: How the Left's Outrage Industry Shuts Down Debate, Manipulates Voters, and Makes America Less Free* (New York: Crown Forum, 2016).
53. Steve Tobak, "The Real Impact of Political Correctness," *Fox Business*, April 19, 2013, http://www.foxbusiness.com/features/2013/04/19/real-impact-political-correctness.html.
54. Kevin D. Williamson, "Yale's Idiot Children," *National Review*, November 10, 2015, http://www.nationalreview.com/yale-free-speech-protest-ironic.
55. Chris Stafford, "Ben Shapiro Slams Political Correctness at MU After Recent Protests," *Missourian*, November 19, 2015, http://www.columbiamissourian.com/news/local/ben-shapiro-slams-political-correctness-at-mu-after-recent-protests/article_8bddae02-8ef7-11e5-96c5-ef3bf7b7a216.html.
56. Robyn Pennacchia, "Ben Shapiro Declared a Social Justice Warrior by People More Racist Than Ben Shapiro," *Gawker*, April 11, 2016, http://wonkette.com/600536/ben-shapiro-declared-a-social-justice-warrior-by-people-more-racist-than-ben-shapiro.
57. E-mail interview with Matt Lewis, October 28, 2016.
58. Scott Alexander, "Anti-Reactionary FAQ," *Slate Star Codex*, October 20, 2013, http://slatestarcodex.com/2013/10/20/the-anti-reactionary-faq/.
59. According to Moldbug: "So: let's put it as bluntly as possible. At present you believe that, in the American Revolution, good triumphed over evil. This is the aforementioned aggregate. We're going to just scoop that right out with the #6 brain spoon. As we

operate, we'll replace it with the actual story of the American Rebellion—in which evil triumphed over good." Mencius Moldbug, "A Gentle Introduction to Unqualified Reservations," *Unqualified Reservations*, January 15, 2009, http://unqualified-reservations.blogspot.com/2009/01/gentle-introduction-to-unqualified_15.html.

60. James Kirchik, "Trump's Terrifying Online Brigades," *Commentary*, May 16, 2016, https://www.commentarymagazine.com/articles/trumps-terrifying-online-brigades/.
61. Mencius Moldbug, "Why I Am Not a White Nationalist," *Unqualified Reservations*, November 22, 2007, http://unqualified-reservations.blogspot.com/2007/11/why-i-am-not-white-nationalist.html.
62. I asked the Alt-Right blogger Lawrence Murray about this overlap, and he said: "Regarding Neo-Reaction or NRx there is some overlap between the two, and I remember years ago coming across the now mostly inactive but in my opinion very insightful RadishMag, though at the same time I was also reading *The Occidental Observer* (which is unambiguously about White identity and nationalism). NRx is more into 'passivism' than the Alt-Right's emphasis on politics and culture-jamming; for more on that you should look into Social Matter. NRx also tends to be more traditionally religious and interested in monarchism." Personal interview, October 29, 2016.
63. E-mail interview with August J. Rush, November 30, 2016.
64. Mencius Moldbug, "Coda," *Unqualified Reservations*, April 18, 2016, http://unqualified-reservations.blogspot.com/2016/04/coda.html.
65. Caitlin Dewey, "The Only Guide to Gamergate You Will Ever Need to Read," *Washington Post*, October 14, 2014, https://www.washingtonpost.com/news/the-intersect/wp/2014/10/14/the-only-guide-to-Gamergate-you-will-ever-need-to-read/.
66. Caitlyn Dewey, "Inside Gamergate's (Successful) Attack on the Media," *Washington Post* October 20, 2016, https://www.washingtonpost.com/news/the-intersect/wp/2014/10/20/inside-gamergates-successful-attack-on-the-media.

1. THE ALT-RIGHT'S GOALS AND PREDECESSORS

67. Max Read, "Did I Kill Gawker," *New York*, August 19, 2016, http://nymag.com/selectall/2016/08/did-i-kill-gawker.html.
68. Ibid.
69. Ian Miles Cheong, "No Hillary, GamerGaters Are Not 'Alt-Right,'" *Heat Street*, September 8, 2016, https://heatst.com/politics/no-hillary-gamergaters-are-not-alt-right/.
70. B.U.G.S. Fighting White Genocide, "The Mantra," http://www.whitakeronline.org/blog/the-white-mantra/.
71. Matt Parrot, "The True Leader of the Alt-Right Is . . ." Traditionalist Youth Network, n.d., http://www.tradyouth.org/2016/08/the-true-leader-of-the-altright/.

2. THE FIRST WAVE OF THE ALT-RIGHT

1. Paul Gottfried, "A Paleo Epitaph," *Taki's Magazine*, April 7, 2008, http://takimag.com/article/a_paleo_epitaph/.
2. Personal interview, October 12, 2016.
3. In a recent article, Gottfried declared, "When she asked me whether I belonged to the Altright, I denied it. The reason was certainly not that I feared that an affirmative answer would cost me my standing as a political theorist or journalist. I have no high status to lose and am now too old to acquire one. The plain truth is I don't have much association beyond a genealogical one and my friendship with some of its contributors to the present Altright. Some of what I see on its websites closely coincide with my views. And (no I won't hide this) I am ideologically closer to Altright commentators than I am to the Never-Trumpers or to the contributors to most establishment Republican websites." Paul Gottfried, "Some Observations from the Man Who Created the Alt-Right," *Front Page Magazine*, August 30, 2016, http://www.frontpagemag.com/fpm/263988/some-observations-man-who-created-alt-right-paul-gottfried.
4. In that same article, he said: "Unfortunately there is this hitch among representatives of Altright. At least some of them show tasteless prankishness and a tendency to say outrageous things

just to shock. I told AP that there are 'moderates' on Altright; and they are the ones who construct the convincing arguments. Unfortunately our leftist (indeed Cultural Marxist) media are more interested in embarrassing the entire Right by quoting the nuttiest remarks made by those identified with the Altright than they are in noticing inconvenient truths. And it's obvious to me that statements that come out of Altright, intended to unsettle blacks, Hispanics, and Jews (but kindly note never the gay lobby), are counterproductive. They do nothing to enhance the credibility of this oppositional force." Ibid.

5. Jacob Siegel, "The Alt-Right's Jewish Godfather," *Tablet*, November 29, 2016, http://www.tabletmag.com/jewish-news-and-politics/218712/spencer-gottfried-alt-right.
6. E-mail correspondence with Paul Gottfried, February 8, 2017.
7. Gottfried, "A Paleo Epitaph."
8. Richard Spencer, "Rotten in Durham," *American Conservative*, February 26, 2007, http://www.theamericanconservative.com/articles/rotten-in-durham/.
9. Todd Seavey, "Debate at Lolita Bar: 'Is Christianity for Wimps?'" ToddSeavey.com, March 1, 2010, http://www.toddseavey.com/2010/03/debate-at-lolita-bar-christianity-for.html.
10. For example, Spencer spoke at the Property and Freedom Society Conference in 2010.
11. "About Us," *Taki's Magazine*, https://web.archive.org/web/20080915160616/http://www.takimag.com/info/about/.
12. F. J. Sarto, "Farewell, Dear Readers," *Taki's Magazine*, January 3, 2008, http://takimag.com/article/farewell_dear_readers/.
13. To my knowledge, the first time Taylor's work was printed in *Taki's Magazine* occurred in 2007. The article in question did not deal explicitly with the issue of race. Jared Taylor, "Primal Moments," *Taki's Magazine*, November 17, 2007, http://takimag.com/article/primal_moments/.
14. John Zmirak, "The Sad Sorority of Skin," *Taki's Magazine*, July 1, 2008, http://takimag.com/article/the_sad_sorority_of_skin/.
15. Richard Spencer, "White Like Us," *Taki's Magazine*, May 22, 2009, http://takimag.com/article/white_like_us/.

16. Richard Spencer, "The End of Rand Paul . . . and Libertarian Populism," *Radix*, February 4, 2016, http://www.radixjournal.com/blog/2016/2/4/the-end-of-rand-paul-and-libertarian-populism.
17. Personal interview with Richard Spencer, October 12, 2016.
18. "National Review's John O'Sullivan: On the Board of Directors of a White Nationalist Group," *Little Green Footballs*, April 17, 2012, http://littlegreenfootballs.com/article/40222_National_Reviews_John_OSullivan-_On_the_Board_of_Directors_of_a_White_Nationalist_Group.
19. Greg Johnson, "The Alt-Right Means White Nationalism . . . or Nothing at All," *Counter-Currents*, August 30, 2016, http://www.counter-currents.com/2016/08/the-alt-right-means-white-nationalism/.
20. Southern Poverty Law Center, "William H. Regnery II," https://www.splcenter.org/fighting-hate/extremist-files/individual/william-h-regnery-ii.
21. Richard Spencer, interview with David Gordon, podcast audio, March 24, 2010, *Radix*, http://www.radixjournal.com/podcast/podcast/273/; Richard Spencer, interview with Thomas E. Woods, podcast audio, March 25, 2010, *Radix*, http://www.radixjournal.com/podcast/podcast/271/; Richard Spencer, interview with E. Christian Kopff, podcast audio, March 12, 2010, http://www.radixjournal.com/podcast/podcast/276/; E. Christian Kopff, "Julius Evola and Radical Traditionalism," *Radix*, February 28, 2010, http://www.radixjournal.com/altright-archive/altright-archive/main/the-magazine/radical-traditionalism.
22. Larry Keller, "Paleocon Starts New Extreme-Right Magazine," *HateWatch*, March 15, 2010, https://www.splcenter.org/hatewatch/2010/03/15/paleocon-starts-new-extreme-right-magazine.
23. Tim Mak, "The 'New' Racist Right," *Frum Forum*, March 8, 2010, https://web.archive.org/web/20160119155933/http://www.frumforum.com/the-new-racist-right/.
24. William Pierce, previously discussed, was perhaps the most prominent exception.
25. Personal interview with Richard Spencer, October 12, 2016.

26. Ibid.
27. Richard Spencer, "The Future of AlternativeRight.com," *Radix*, May 3, 2012, http://www.radixjournal.com/altright-archive/altright-archive/fundraising/the-future-of-alternativerightcom.
28. "Greg Johnson interviews Richard Spencer on Radixjournal.com," *Counter-Currents*, January 14, 2015, http://www.counter-currents.com/2014/01/greg-johnson-interviews-richard-spencer-on-radixjournal-com/.
29. *Radix* Journal's Facebook page, December 27, 2013, https://www.facebook.com/radixjournal/photos/a.567912143291594.1073741829.555555737860568/568380836578058/?type=3&theater.
30. Richard Spencer, "What I Was Thinking [podcast]," *Radix*, January 23, 2014, https://web.archive.org/web/20150202064456/http://www.radixjournal.com/vanguard-radio/2014/1/3/what-was-i-thinking.
31. E-mail correspondence with Jared Taylor, July 25, 2016.
32. Southern Poverty Law Center, "A Guide to the Alt-Right, Modern White Supremacists Bolstering Trump," *Alternet*, August 28, 2016, http://www.alternet.org/right-wing/guide-alt-right.
33. Andy Nowicki, "Nameless Podcast: Miscegenation and the Alt-Right," *Alternative Right*, December 21, 2015, http://alternative-right.blogspot.com/2015/12/miscegenation-and-alt-right.html.

3. THE ALT-RIGHT RETURNS

1. Anti-Defamation League, "14/88," http://www.adl.org/combating-hate/hate-on-display/c/1488.html.
2. Personal interview with Richard Spencer, October 12, 2016.
3. E-mail interview with Lawrence Murray, October 28, 2016.
4. E-mail interview with Jazzhands McFeels, November 11, 2016.
5. Andrew Anglin, "A Normie's Guide to the Alt-Right," *Daily Stormer*, August 31, 2016, http://www.dailystormer.com/a-normies-guide-to-the-alt-right/.
6. Rosie Gray, "How 2015 Fueled the Rise of the Freewheeling, White Nationalist Alt Right Movement," *Buzzfeed*, December 27,

2015, http://www.buzzfeed.com/rosiegray/how-2015-fueled-the-rise-of-the-freewheeling-white-nationali/.

7. Clear Above, "Tips for Trolls," *Right Stuff*, February 2, 2016, http://therightstuff.biz/2016/02/02/tips-for-trolls/.
8. Adam Selene, "The Essential TRS Troll Guide, Part 1," *Right Stuff*, January 16, 2015, http://therightstuff.biz/2015/01/16/the-essential-trs-troll-guide-part-1/.
9. Olivia Nuzzi, "How Pepe the Frog Became a Nazi Trump Supporter and Alt-Right Symbol," *Daily Beast*, May 26, 2016, http://www.thedailybeast.com/articles/2016/05/26/how-pepe-the-frog-became-a-nazi-trump-supporter-and-alt-right-symbol.html.
10. Jonah Bennett, "Here's How Two Twitter Pranksters Convinced the World That Pepe the Frog Meme Is Just a Front for White Nationalism," *Daily Caller*, September 14, 2016, http://dailycaller.com/2016/09/14/heres-how-two-twitter-pranksters-convinced-the-world-that-pepe-the-frog-meme-is-just-a-front-for-white-nationalism/.
11. Ben Schreckinger, "White Nationalists Plot Election Day Show of Force," *Politico*, November 2, 2016, http://www.politico.com/story/2016/11/suppress-black-vote-trump-campaign-230616.
12. Jonah Bennett, "CONFIRMED: Politico Ran Laughably Fake Story on Alt-Right Voter Suppression," *Daily Caller*, November 3, 2016, http://dailycaller.com/2016/11/03/alt-right-group-reveals-in-depth-how-the-black-voter-suppression-plan-causing-hysteria-was-a-complete-troll/.
13. Murdoch Murdoch, "Meme Magic," YouTube, posted September 3, 2016, https://www.youtube.com/watch?v=sTy3mJZXf_0.
14. E-mail interview with Jazzhands McFeels, November 11, 2016.
15. I say supposedly because the evidence that there is a long-running, systematic "generation gap" in politics is actually rather weak.
16. Lauren M. Fox, "'We Want to Change the World': Inside a White Supremacist Conference Aimed at Millennials," *Salon*, October 29, 2013, http://www.salon.com/2013/10/29/white_separatists_are_afraid_of_the_future/.

17. Southern Poverty Law Center, "Youth Turn Out in Large Numbers for NPI's Rainbow Racist Gathering," November 3, 2015, https://www.splcenter.org/hatewatch/2015/11/03/youth-turn-out-large-numbers-npi%E2%80%99s-rainbow-racist-gathering.
18. Interview with Richard Spencer, October 12, 2016.
19. Greg Johnson, "The Boomerang Generation: Connecting with Our Proletariat," *Counter-Currents*, August 27, 2016, http://www.counter-currents.com/2013/08/the-counter-currents-2013-summer-fundraiser-2/.
20. E-mail with Lawrence Murray, October 28, 2016.
21. Ibid.
22. This is generally the argument that Lawrence Murray made when I asked him about his movement: "With older White nationalism some people like to use the terms WN 1.0 and WN 2.0 to refer to the 'pre-Alt-Right' White nationalism movement versus the current year's edition. I myself had never heard of Pierce or Duke for example until becoming involved with the Alt-Right. I think a major distinction is that many younger White people in the United States have never known a White nation-state and for them it is now a dream not unlike 19th century Zionism. With WN 1.0 you had a very Southern-centered movement that in many ways was reacting against racial integration and communism, and which objectively failed. But they remembered a country where White rule was a genuine construct and you had nakedly pro-White policies such as the pre-1965 immigration laws. WN 2.0, or the Alt-Right variety of White nationalism, has emerged in a very different context, and it should come as no surprise that you have people coming out of California and New York now just as much as places like Tennessee and Missouri." Ibid.
23. Richard Dawkins, *The Selfish Gene* (New York: Oxford University Press, 1976), 206–207.
24. Keegan Hankes, "SPLC Analysis: Small Community of Extremists on Twitter Responsible for Majority of Message," Southern Poverty Law Center, October 31, 2016, https://www.splcenter.org/hatewatch/2016/10/31/splc-analysis-small-community-extremists-twitter-responsible-majority-message.

25. For just a sense of how pervasive this campaign was, days before the election #draftourdaughters posters were placed on public boards throughout the University of Alabama.
26. Cooper Fleishman and Anthony Smith, "'Coincidence Detector': The Google Chrome Extension White Supremacists Use to Track Jews," *Mic*, June 2, 2016, https://mic.com/articles/145105/coincidence-detector-the-google-extension-white-supremacists-use-to-track-jews/.
27. Andrew Anglin, "Doing It Wrong: The Jews Echo Themselves in an Attempt to Reverse-Meme the Alt-Right," *Daily Stormer*, June 3, 2016, http://www.dailystormer.com/doing-it-wrong-the-jews-echo-themselves-in-an-attempt-to-reverse-meme-the-alt-right/.
28. For just one example, the following article was published at *TRS*: Wolfie James, "How to Red Pill Your Woman," *Right Stuff*, November 22, 2016, http://therightstuff.biz/2016/11/22/how-to-red-pill-your-woman/.
29. E-mail interview with Henry Olson, November 28, 2016.
30. Matthew Sheffield, "Meet Moon Man: The Alt-Right's Racist Rap Sensation, Borrowed from 1980s McDonald's Ads," *Salon*, October 25, 2016, http://www.salon.com/2016/10/25/meet-moon-man-the-alt-rights-new-racist-rap-sensation-borrowed-from-1980s-mcdonalds-ads/.
31. Derrick L. Cogburn and Fatima K. Espinoza-Vasquez, "From Networked Nominee to Networked Nation: Examining the Impact of Web 2.0 and Social Media on Political Participation and Civic Engagement in the 2008 Obama Campaign," *Journal of Political Marketing* 10 (2011): 189–213.
32. Douglas Haddow, "Meme Warfare: How the Power of Mass Replication Has Poisoned the US Election," *Guardian*, November 4, 2016, https://www.theguardian.com/us-news/2016/nov/04/political-memes-2016-election-hillary-clinton-donald-trump.
33. Matthew W. Hughey and Jessie Daniels, "Racist Comments at Online News Sites: A Methodological Dilemma for Discourse Analysis," *Media, Culture, and Society* 35 (2013): 332–333.
34. "Advanced Meme Warfare /cfg/," Pastebin, July 6, 2016, http://pastebin.com/hack9Z6G.

35. Ibid.
36. These lists often include what appear to be the home addresses of these journalists, and for that reason I will not provide them here.
37. E-mail interview with August J. Rush, November 30, 2016.

4. THE ALT-RIGHT ATTACK ON THE CONSERVATIVE MOVEMENT

1. One conservative essayist correctly noted: "Most on the Alt-Right do not only reject the 'conservative Establishment' or some other contemporary bogeyman; they also reject the ideals of classical liberalism as such." Ian Tuttle, "The Racist Moral Rot of the Alt-Right," *National Review*, April 5, 2016, http://www.nationalreview.com/article/433650/alt-rights-racism-moral-rot.
2. For a useful discussion of this strategy from the time of its inception, see Kevin P. Phillips, *The Emerging Republican Majority* (New Rochelle, N.Y.: Arlington House, 1969).
3. For an excellent argument that demographic changes will ultimately doom a Republican Party dependent on middle-class white Christians, see John B. Judis and Ruy Teixeira, *The Emerging Democratic Majority* (New York: Lisa Drew/Scribner, 2002).
4. Ellison Lodge, "The White People Party," *Taki's Magazine*, August 24, 2009, http://takimag.com/article/the_white_people_party/.
5. Alfred W. Clark, "What is a #Cuckservative?" *Occam's Razor* , July 15, 2015, https://occamsrazormag.wordpress.com/2015/07/15/what-is-a-cuckservative-nrx/.
6. Alan Rappeport, "From the Right, a New Slur for GOP Candidates," *New York Times*, August 13, 2015, http://www.nytimes.com/2015/08/13/us/from-the-right-a-new-slur-for-gop-candidates.html.
7. Jeet Heer, "Conservatives Are Holding a Conversation About Race," *New Republic*, July 26, 2015, https://newrepublic.com

/article/122372/conservatives-are-holding-conversation-about-race.

8. Matt Lewis, "Twitter's Right-Wing Civil War," *Daily Beast*, September 28, 2015, http://www.thedailybeast.com/articles/2015/07/28/twitter-s-right-wing-civil-war.html.
9. Erick Erickson, "'Cuckservative' Is a Racist Slur and an Attack on Evangelical Christians," *RedState*, July 29, 2015, http://www.redstate.com/erick/2015/07/29/cuckservative-is-a-racist-slur-and-an-attack-on-evangelical-christians/.
10. Rush Limbaugh, "Trump Was Supposed to Be Gone by Now [Transcript]," *Rush Limbaugh Show*, July 22, 2015, http://www.rushlimbaugh.com/daily/2015/07/22/trump_was_supposed_to_be_gone_by_now.
11. Milo Yiannopoulos, "'Cuckservative' Is a Gloriously Effective Insult That Should Not Be Slurred, Demonized, or Ridiculed," *Breitbart*, July 28, 2015, http://www.breitbart.com/big-government/2015/07/28/cuckservative-is-a-gloriously-effective-insult-that-should-not-be-slurred-demonised-or-ridiculed/.
12. Vox Day and John Red Eagle, *Cuckservative: How "Conservatives" Betrayed America* (Kouvola, Finland: Castalia House, 2015).
13. Ibid., Kindle location 148–149.
14. Clear Above, "Lessons Learned from #Cuckservative," *Right Stuff*, October 23, 2015, http://therightstuff.biz/2015/10/23/lessons-learned-from-cuckservative/. The Overton Window is the range of acceptable political opinions within a society, marking the line at which a person can be labeled an extremist rather than within the mainstream. Ben Garrison is a well-known far-right cartoonist.
15. Li Tan, Suma Ponnam, Patrick Gillham, Bob Edwards, and Erik Johnson, "Analyzing the Impact of Social Media on Social Movements: A Computational Study on Twitter and the Occupy Wall Street Movement," in *Advances in Social Networks Analysis and Mining (ASONAM), 2013 IEEE/ACM International Conference* (IEEE, 2013), 1259–1266.
16. "Ten Most Harmful Books of the Nineteenth and Twentieth Century," *Human Events*, May 31, 2005, http://humanevents.com

/2005/05/31/ten-most-harmful-books-of-the-19th-and-20th-centuries/.

17. For just one of many examples of Alt-Right writers explaining their fondness for Nietzsche, see Michael McGregor, "A Festival for Slaves," *Radix*, April 19, 2014, http://www.radixjournal.com/blog/2014/4/19/a-festival-of-slave-morality.
18. Gal. 3:28. King James Version.
19. Jack Jenkins, "The New Religion of Choice for White Supremacists," *ThinkProgress,* November 13, 2016, https://thinkprogress.org/the-new-religion-of-choice-for-white-supremacists-8af2a69a3440.
20. This is not a point that has been lost on all elements of the irreligious Alt-Right, including some of the most hostile anti-Semites. For an example of a non-Christian who appreciates the anti-Semitic elements of Christian history, and even of contemporary Christianity, see Andrew Anglin, "Looking at Christianity Objectively," *Daily Stormer*, April 10, 2013, http://www.dailystormer.com/looking-at-christianity-objectively/.
21. Randall Balmer, "The Real Origins of the Religious Right," *Salon*, May 27, 2014, http://www.politico.com/magazine/story/2014/05/religious-right-real-origins-107133.
22. Southern Baptist Convention, "On Immigration and the Gospel," 2011, http://www.sbc.net/resolutions/1213.
23. David Roach, "SBC Blog," *Baptist Press*, June 14, 2016, http://www.bpnews.net/47028/sbc-blog.
24. Ethics and Religious Liberty Commission of the Southern Baptist Convention, "Resolution 7: On Sensitivity and Unity Regarding the Confederate Battle Flag," June 14, 2016, http://erlc.com/resource-library/articles/resolution-7-on-sensitivity-and-unity-regarding-the-confederate-battle-flag.
25. Hunter Wallace, "Russell Moore: Can the Religious Right Be Saved?" *Occidental Dissent*, October 25, 2016, http://www.occidentaldissent.com/2016/10/25/russell-moore-can-the-religious-right-be-saved/.
26. Massimo Faggioli, "Pope Francis Refuses to Associate Islam with Violence," *Huffington Post*, August 3, 2016, http://www

.huffingtonpost.com/massimo-faggioli/pope-francis-refuses-to-associate_b_11307106.html.

27. Aylmer Fisher, "The Pro-Life Temptation," *Radix*, April 8, 2016, http://www.radixjournal.com/journal/2016/4/8/the-pro-life-temptation.
28. Gregory Hood, *Waking Up from the American Dream* (San Francisco: Counter-Currents, 2016).
29. For one example, see Gregory Hood, "Why Christianity Can't Save Us," *Counter-Currents*, July 31, 2013, http://www.counter-currents.com/2013/07/why-christianity-cant-save-us/.
30. E-mail interview with Gregory Hood, October 19, 2016.
31. "GOP Consultant Rick Wilson to MSNBC: Trump Supporters 'Childless Single Men Who Masturbate to Anime,'" *Breitbart*, January 20, 2016, http://www.breitbart.com/video/2016/01/20/gop-consultant-rick-wilson-to-msnbc-trump-supporters-childless-single-men-who-masturbate-to-anime/.
32. Jamie Weinstein, "Rick Wilson: Trump Oppo Coming That Could 'End the Race,' Make Even Ardent Trumpers Go 'Whoa,'" *Daily Caller*, October 17, 2016, http://dailycaller.com/2016/10/17/rick-wilson-trump-oppo-coming-that-could-end-the-race-make-even-ardent-trumpers-go-whoa/.
33. Bethany Mandel, "My Trump Tweets Earned Me So Many Anti-Semitic Haters I Bought a Gun," *Forward*, March 21, 2016, http://forward.com/opinion/336159/my-trump-tweets-earned-me-so-many-anti-semitic-haters-that-i-bought-a-gun/.
34. David French, "The Price I've Paid for Opposing Donald Trump," *National Review Online*, October 21, 2016, http://www.nationalreview.com/article/441319/donald-trump-alt-right-internet-abuse-never-trump-movement.
35. Ibid.
36. Erick Erickson, "The GOP After Donald Trump," *New York Times*, October 14, 2016, http://www.nytimes.com/2016/10/14/opinion/erick-erickson-the-gop-after-donald-trump.html.
37. Mandel, "My Trump Tweets."
38. Ibid.

4. THE ALT-RIGHT ATTACK ON THE CONSERVATIVE MOVEMENT

39. E-mail interview with Matt Lewis, October 28, 2016.
40. Hawley, *Right-Wing Critics of American Conservatism*, 37–73.
41. "Why the South Must Prevail," *National Review* 4, no. 7 (1957): 148–149; Theodore Johnson, "Civil Rights Republicanism: How the GOP Can Appeal to Black Voters, and Why It Should," *National Review*, November 2, 2016, https://www.nationalreview.com/nrd/articles/425617/civil-rights-republicanism.
42. *National Review* made it clear that its brand of conservatism had no shared philosophical premises with Rand's objectivist philosophy when it published a negative review of *Atlas Shrugged*. Whittaker Chambers, "Big Sister Is Watching You," *National Review*, December 28, 1957.
43. Ed Morrissey, "Hewitt, Goldberg: The 'Core Alt-Right' Needs to Be Driven from Conservative Ranks," *Hot Air*, August 31, 2016, http://hotair.com/archives/2016/08/31/hewitt-goldberg-core-alt-right-needs-driven-conservative-ranks/.
44. Kenneth P. Vogel, "Behind Trump's CPAC Deal Gone Bad," *Politico*, March 4, 2016, http://www.politico.com/story/2016/03/donald-trump-cpac-deal-dispute-220285.
45. National Review Symposium, "Against Trump," *National Review Online*, January 21, 2016, http://c7.nrostatic.com/article/430126/donald-trump-conservatives-oppose-nomination.
46. Ibid.
47. Kevin D. Williamson, "Nationalists for a Smaller America," *National Review*, October 5, 2016, http://www.nationalreview.com/article/440710/trumps-nationalism-about-reduced-global-trade-engagement.
48. Ramesh Ponnuru and Rich Lowry, "For Love of Country: A Defense of Nationalism," *National Review*, February 20, 2017, https://www.nationalreview.com/magazine/2017-02-20-0000/donald-trump-inauguration-speech-and-nationalism.
49. For a good explanation of how Trump's win divided conservatives, see Tevi Troy, "How Trump Split Conservatives Three Ways," *Politico*, February 25, 2017, http://www.politico.com/magazine/story/2017/02/how-trump-split-conservatives-three-ways-214826.

50. Harry Cheadle, "Trump's CPAC Speech Showed That Trumpism Has Killed Conservatism," *Vice*, February 24, 2017, https://www.vice.com/en_us/article/trumps-cpac-speech-showed-that-trumpism-has-killed-conservatism.
51. For a detailed discussion of these recent examples, see Hawley, *Right-Wing Critics of American Conservatism*, chap. 2.

5. THE ALT-RIGHT AND THE 2016 ELECTION

1. Russell Goldman, "John McCain Border Shift: 'Complete Danged Fence,'" *ABC News*, May 11, 2010, http://abcnews.go.com/Politics/john-mccain-immigration-reversal-complete-danged-fence/story?id=10616090.
2. William Horton was a murderer imprisoned in Massachusetts. In 1986, while Michael Dukakis was the governor of that state, Horton was released as part of a weekend-furlough program. While on furlough, he committed additional violent crimes. During the 1988 presidential race between Bush and Dukakis, Bush repeatedly referenced this event, and advertisements that referenced Dukakis's record on crime were widely perceived as racist. Roger Simon, "How a Murderer and Rapist Became the Bush Campaign's Most Valuable Player," *Baltimore Sun*, November 11, 1990, http://articles.baltimoresun.com/1990-11-11/features/1990315149_1_willie-horton-fournier-michael-dukakis.
3. Henry Barbour, Sally Bradshaw, Ari Fleischer, Zori Fonallesas, and Glenn McCall, "The Growth and Opportunity Project," Republican National Committee, 2013, http://goproject.gop.com/.
4. Matt Parrot, "Let's Not Be Trump's Chumps," *Counter-Currents*, July 10, 2015, http://www.counter-currents.com/2015/07/lets-not-be-trumps-chumps/.
5. Greg Johnson, "2015: The Year in White Nationalism," *Counter-Currents*, December 31, 2015, http://www.counter-currents.com/2015/12/2015-the-year-in-white-nationalism/.

6. Will Rahn, "Inside the White Supremacists' Halloween Bash," *Daily Beast*, November 2, 2015, http://www.thedailybeast.com/articles/2015/11/02/inside-the-white-supremacists-halloween-bash.html.
7. Daniel Marans, "How Trump Is Inspiring a New Generation of White Nationalists," *Huffington Post*, March 7, 2016, http://www.huffingtonpost.com/entry/trump-white-nationalists_us_56dd99c2e4b0ffe6f8e9ee7c.
8. The Southern Poverty Law Center has a page dedicated to Paul, where it states: "A scathing critic of 'cultural Marxism'—once an actual school of socialist thought but now a bogeyman to radical rightists who see it as a secret conspiracy to destroy Western society from within—Paul Ramsey is a white nationalist who posts Internet videos of himself talking to the camera under the screen name of Ramzpaul. Ramsey calls himself a "satirist," a kind of far-right Jon Stewart, but he is more importantly an ideologue and a hero to much of the radical right. Since 2009, he has uploaded hundreds of liberal-loathing, feminist-bashing, and racial separatist-supporting vlogs, or video blogs, to his personal YouTube channel, typically at the rate of three a week. By 2014, his channel had close to 20,000 subscribers, and his vlogs were being frequently posted to unapologetically white supremacist websites like Vanguard News Network and Stormfront." Southern Poverty Law Center, "About Paul Ray Ramsey," https://www.splcenter.org/fighting-hate/extremist-files/individual/paul-ray-ramsey.
9. Tal Kopan, "Donald Trump Retweets 'White Genocide' Twitter User," *CNN*, January 22, 2016, http://www.cnn.com/2016/01/22/politics/donald-trump-retweet-white-genocide/.
10. Donald J. Trump, Twitter post, October 13, 2015, 1:53 a.m., https://twitter.com/realdonaldtrump/status/653856168402681856.
11. Melissa Cronin, "Donald Trump Will Never Stop Retweeting White Supremacists," *Gawker*, February 27, 2016, http://gawker.com/donald-trump-will-never-stop-retweeting-white-supremaci-1761721723.

12. Team Fix, Abby Olheiser, and Caitlin Dewey, "Hillary Clinton's Alt-Right Speech, Annotated," *Washington Post*, August 25, 2016, https://www.washingtonpost.com/news/the-fix/wp/2016/08/25/hillary-clintons-alt-right-speech-annotated/.
13. Ibid.
14. Michelle Goldberg, "Hillary Clinton's Alt-Right Speech Isolated and Destroyed Donald Trump," *Slate*, August 25, 2016, http://www.slate.com/articles/news_and_politics/politics/2016/08/how_hillary_clinton_s_alt_right_speech_isolated_and_destroyed_donald_trump.html.
15. Matt Lewis, Twitter post, August 25, 2016, 12:35 p.m., https://twitter.com/mattklewis/status/768894560961298432.
16. Amanda Carpenter, Twitter post, August 25, 2016, 12:27 p.m., https://twitter.com/amandacarpenter/status/768892612371746816.
17. Amanda Carpenter, "Why Hillary Gave the Alt-Right Speech," *Conservative Review*, August 26, 2016, https://www.conservativereview.com/commentary/2016/08/why-hillary-gave-the-alt-right-speech.
18. Southern Poverty Law Center, "About Alex Jones," https://www.splcenter.org/fighting-hate/extremist-files/individual/alex-jones.
19. Tim Stanley, "Donald Trump, Steve Bannon, and the Alt-Right Conspiracy Myth," *Telegraph*, August 27, 2016, http://www.telegraph.co.uk/news/2016/08/27/donald-trump-steve-bannon-and-the-alt-right-conspiracy-myth/.
20. LeagueOfTheNorth, "No Bad Press: Media Damage Control and the Alt-Right," *Right Stuff*, September 21, 2016, http://therightstuff.biz/2016/09/21/no-bad-press-media-damage-control-the-alt-right/.
21. Zeiger, "Interest in the Alt-Right Exploding," *Daily Stormer*, August 29, 2016, http://www.dailystormer.com/interest-in-the-alt-right-exploding/.
22. Lawrence Murray, "Now I Am Become President, Leader of the Free World," *Right Stuff*, November 9, 2015, http://therightstuff.biz/2016/11/09/now-i-am-become-president-leader-of-the-free-world/.

23. Michael W. Chapman and Eric Scheiner, "Trump on Border: 'We're Going to Build a Wall,' It 'Will Go Up So Fast Your Head Will Spin,'" CNSNews.com, November 15, 2016, http://www.cnsnews.com/news/article/michael-w-chapman/trump-border-were-going-build-wall-dont-worry-it-will-go-so-fast-your.
24. David M. Jackson, "Trump Speaks with Putin by Phone," *USA Today*, November 15, 2016, http://www.usatoday.com/story/news/politics/onpolitics/2016/11/14/donald-trump-vladimir-putin-phone-call-kremlin/93809234/.
25. "Full Text of Trump's Executive Order on Seven-Nation Ban, Refugee Suspension," *CNN*, January 28, 2017, http://www.cnn.com/2017/01/28/politics/text-of-trump-executive-order-nation-ban-refugees/.
26. Ronald Radosh, "Steve Bannon, Trump's Top Guy, Told Me He Was 'a Leninist' Who Wants to 'Destroy the State,'" *Daily Beast*, August 22, 2016, http://www.thedailybeast.com/articles/2016/08/22/steve-bannon-trump-s-top-guy-told-me-he-was-a-leninist.html.
27. Tory Scot, "Twist the Knife," *Right Stuff*, November 11, 2016, http://therightstuff.biz/2016/11/11/twist-the-knife/.
28. Spencer Quinn, "We Need to Move: An Alt Right Take on the 2016 Election," *Counter-Currents*, November 16, 2016, http://www.counter-currents.com/2016/11/we-need-to-move/.
29. Sarah Posner, "How Donald Trump's New Campaign Chief Created an Online Haven for White Nationalists," *Mother Jones*, August 22, 2016, http://www.motherjones.com/politics/2016/08/stephen-bannon-donald-trump-alt-right-breitbart-news.
30. Josh Harkinson, "The Dark History of the White House Aides Who Crafted Trump's 'Muslim Ban,'" *Mother Jones*, January 30, 2017, http://www.motherjones.com/politics/2017/01/stephen-bannon-miller-trump-refugee-ban-islamophobia-white-nationalist.
31. Josh Harkinson, "Trump's Newest Senior Adviser Seen as a White Nationalist Ally," *Mother Jones*, December 14, 2016, http://www.motherjones.com/politics/2016/12/trumps-newest-senior-adviser-seen-ally-white-nationalists.

32. Ibid.
33. Richard Spencer, "Stephen Miller and Me," *AltRight.com*, February 1, 2016, http://www.altright.com/2017/02/01/stephen-miller-and-me/.
34. Tim Mak, "The Troublemaker Behind Donald Trump's Words," *Daily Beast*, January 19, 2017, http://www.thedailybeast.com/articles/2017/01/19/the-troublemaker-behind-donald-trump-s-words.html.
35. Scott Greer, "Conservatives Defend Stephen Miller: A 'Brilliant and Courageous' Man," *Daily Caller*, February 1, 2017, http://dailycaller.com/2017/02/01/conservatives-defend-stephen-miller-a-brilliant-and-courageous-man/.
36. Ryan Lenz, "The Godfather," Southern Poverty Law Center, May 24, 2014, https://www.splcenter.org/fighting-hate/intelligence-report/2014/godfather.
37. For example, the Maoist Freedom Road Socialist Organization was excited by the Sanders campaign. Cazembe, "Crush Trump! Build Our Movements!" Freedom Road Socialist Organization, August 3, 2016, http://freedomroad.org/2016/08/crush-trump-build-our-movements/.
38. For an example, see Jamelle Bouie, "Government by White Nationalism Is Upon Us," *Slate*, February 6, 2017, http://www.slate.com/articles/news_and_politics/cover_story/2017/02/government_by_white_nationalism_is_upon_us.html.
39. "Ads Compare Bush to Hitler," *Washington Times*, January 5, 2004, http://www.washingtontimes.com/news/2004/jan/5/20040105-114507-1007r/.
40. Jonah Goldberg, *Liberal Fascism: The Secret History of the American Left, from Mussolini to the Politics of Meaning* (New York: Doubleday, 2007).
41. The entire NPI conference can now be viewed online. "Red Ice NPI Coverage," *Radix*, November 30, 2016, http://www.radixjournal.com/blog/2016/11/30/red-ice-npi-converage [*sic*].
42. Richard Spencer, "Long Live the Emperor," *Radix*, November 21, 2016, http://www.radixjournal.com/journal/2016/11/21/long-live-the-emperor.

43. Ibid.
44. Daniel Lombroso and Yoni Applebaum, "'Hail Trump!': White Nationalists Salute the President Elect," *Atlantic*, November 21, 2016, http://www.theatlantic.com/politics/archive/2016/11/richard-spencer-speech-npi/508379/.
45. There are more examples of this than can be named here, but see the *New York Times* for just one of these articles. Joseph Goldstein, "Alt-Right Gathering Exults in Trump Election with Nazi-Era Salute," *New York Times*, November 20, 2016, http://www.nytimes.com/2016/11/21/us/alt-right-salutes-donald-trump.html.
46. Brent Griffiths, "Trump Disavows the Alt-Right," *Politico*, November 22, 2016, http://www.politico.com/blogs/donald-trump-administration/2016/11/did-trump-energize-alt-right-231749.
47. Kristoffer Ronneberg, "Jared Taylor," *Soundcloud*, November 23, 2016, https://soundcloud.com/ristofferonneberg/jared-taylor.
48. Ibid.
49. RamZPaul, "Alt-Right—RIP," YouTube video, November 23, 2016, https://www.youtube.com/watch?v=n8HBLX_khwQ.
50. Greg Johnson, "The Alt-Right: Obituary for a Brand," *Counter-Currents*, November 29, 2016, http://www.counter-currents.com/2016/11/the-alt-right-obituary-for-a-brand/print/.
51. Andrew Anglin, "Hero Spencer Under Brutal Assault by Cuckolded Faggots," *Daily Stormer*, November 23, 2016, http://www.dailystormer.com/hero-spencer-under-brutal-assault-by-cuckolded-faggots/.
52. Richard Spencer, "Roman Holiday," *Radix*, November 24, 2016, http://www.radixjournal.com/blog/2016/11/24/roman-holidayspencer-statement.
53. Ibid.
54. John Daniszewski, "Writing About the 'Alt-Right,'" *Associated Press*, November 28, 2016, https://blog.ap.org/behind-the-news/writing-about-the-alt-right.

6. THE "ALT-LITE"

1. Jack Hunter, May 30, 2009 (6:29 p.m.) comment on Clark Stooksbury, "No Thanks," *American Conservative*, May 30, 2009, http://www.theamericanconservative.com/2009/05/30/no-thanks/.
2. Hunter wrote in August 2016: "For at least a year, a small army of online right-wing trolls—who refer to themselves as the 'alt-right'—has attacked anyone who dared challenge Trump. They use some of the most racist and anti-Semitic language imaginable. N-words (directed at blacks), K-words (directed at Jews) and Holocaust and gas chamber 'jokes' are commonplace. So are grand declarations about defending the 'White race'—and White is almost always capitalised in the alt-right world. And they're not just anti-minority, but anti-feminist, anti-egalitarian and anti-democracy. 'Fascist' isn't a pejorative but a debatable form of government to alt-righters and to many, a positive one." Jack Hunter, "How Donald Trump Shacked Up with the Alt-Right," *Spectator*, August 23, 2016, http://blogs.spectator.co.uk/2016/08/donald-trump-alt-right/.
3. Mike Ma, "Neo-Nazi Site 'Daily Stormer' Protests Milo at University of Alabama," *Breitbart*, October 11, 2016, http://www.breitbart.com/milo/2016/10/11/anti-milo-daily-stormer-pamphlet-makes-rounds-university-alabama-event/.
4. Greg Piper, "Milo Yiannopoulos Gives a Boring Speech After University of Alabama Cancels $7,000 Speech Tax," *College Fix*, October 13, 2016, http://www.thecollegefix.com/post/29448/.
5. John K. Wilson, *The Myth of Political Correctness: The Conservative Attack on Higher Education* (Durham, N.C.: Duke University Press, 1995).
6. For one example, see Madeleine Sweet, "Please Shut Up About Milo and 'Free Speech,'" *Huffington Post*, July 26, 2016, http://www.huffingtonpost.com/entry/please-shut-up-about-milo-and-free-speech_us_57926293e4b0a86259d13bf4.
7. Ben Kew, "New York Times Magazine Q&A: Milo Yiannopoulos 'Doesn't Have Feelings,'" *Breitbart*, May 4, 2016, http://www

.breitbart.com/milo/2016/05/04/new-york-times-qa-milo-yiannopoulos-doesnt-feelings/.

8. Allum Bokhari and Milo Yiannopoulos, "An Establishment Conservative's Guide to the Alt-Right," *Breitbart*, March 29, 2016, http://www.breitbart.com/tech/2016/03/29/an-establishment-conservatives-guide-to-the-alt-right/.
9. Ibid.
10. Milo Yiannopoulos, "Full Text: Milo on How Feminism Hurts Men and Women," *Breitbart*, October 7, 2016, 2017, http://www.breitbart.com/milo/2016/10/07/full-text-milo-feminism-auburn/.
11. Milo Yiannopoulos, "Full Text: 10 Things Milo Hates About Islam," *Breitbart*, September 27, 2016, http://www.breitbart.com/milo/2016/09/27/10-things-milo-hates-islam/.
12. Stephen Piggott, "Is Breitbart.com Becoming the Media Arm of the 'Alt-Right'?" Southern Poverty Law Center, April 28, 2016, https://www.splcenter.org/hatewatch/2016/04/28/breitbartcom-becoming-media-arm-alt-right.
13. Gavin McInnes, "Love Your Fellow Hater," *Taki's Magazine* October 6, 2016, http://takimag.com/article/love_your_fellow_hater_gavin_mcinnes#axzz4Q0022tBi.
14. A writer at the website Antifa.net made just this point: "What a fascist ideological current needs to become a movement is a way to crossover. To gain entry into the culture, into public discourse, into the collective consciousness. Over the years, fascism, with its various ideological positions like innate human inequality and essentialized identities, has found people that could bridge the edge of acceptability to their world of racism. In the 1980s and 1990s this was largely made up of Paleoconservatism, where the high water mark was people like Pat Buchanan. It also took the form of the broader conspiracy theorist world, which mainstreamed ideas like the Jews being responsible for 9/11 or the notion that the Holocaust was a Jewish fabrication. Today, the Alt Right is the latest successful branding of the ongoing fascist movement, and it simply brings white nationalism into the current world of memes and ironic hashtags. Its massive growth has come, largely, from an

internal culture where someone can rise to the status of subcultural celebrity without ever being known to the mainstream. Within this world they have still had to find ways of mainstreaming their message, and they have done this by cozying up to people who make many of their larger political points without all of the baggage." "Meet the Alt Lite, the People Mainstreaming the Alt Right's White Nationalism, Antifa.net, March 11, 2016, http://www.antifa.net/meet-the-alt-lite-the-people-mainstreaming-the-alt-rights-white-nationalism/.

15. Besides Yiannopoulos, Mike Cernovich has also been inaccurately labeled as an "Alt-Right leader." Alex Griswold, "Alt-Right in Civil War After Prominent Leader Disinvited From Pro-Trump 'DeploraBall,'" *Mediaite*, December 27, 2016, http://www.mediaite.com/online/alt-right-in-civil-war-after-prominent-leader-disinvited-from-pro-trump-deploraball/.
16. Andrew Anglin, "Stormer Book Club Crusade: The Final Solution to the Milo Problem," *Daily Stormer*, September 27, 2016, http://www.dailystormer.com/stormer-book-club-crusade-the-final-solution-to-the-milo-problem/.
17. Andrew Anglin, "Holy Crusade: Alt-Right to Boycott Breitbart Until Milo Is Removed," *Daily Stormer*, September 29, 2016, http://www.dailystormer.com/holy-crusade-alt-right-to-boycott-breitbart-until-milo-is-removed/.
18. Andrew Anglin, "Kike-Lover Lauren Southern Should Shut Her Slut Mouth," *Daily Stormer*, September 19, 2016, http://www.dailystormer.com/kike-lover-lauren-southern-should-shut-her-slut-mouth/.
19. Tory Scot, "Milo Isn't One of Us," *Right Stuff*, May 6, 2016, http://therightstuff.biz/2016/05/06/milo-isnt-one-of-us/.
20. Alexander Hart, "Entryists or Entry Point? In Defense of the Alt-Lite," *American Renaissance*, August 30, 2016, http://www.amren.com/news/2016/08/entryists-or-entry-point-in-defense-of-the-alt-lite/.
21. Hunter Wallace, "The Alt-Lite Isn't Going Anywhere," *Occidental Dissent*, December 1, 2016, http://www.occidentaldissent.com/2016/12/01/the-alt-lite-isnt-going-anywhere/.

22. Personal interview with Richard Spencer, October 12, 2016.
23. Greg Johnson, "The Alt-Right Means White Nationalism . . . or Nothing at All," *Counter-Currents*, August 20, 2016, http://www.counter-currents.com/2016/08/the-alt-right-means-white-nationalism/.
24. Greg Johnson, "Interview on White Nationalism and the Alt-Right," *Counter-Currents*, October 19, 2016, http://www.counter-currents.com/2016/10/interview-on-white-nationalism-and-the-alt-right/.
25. Specifically, he said: "And yet that is exactly what some conservatives seem intent on doing. For example, my friend Hugh Hewitt, the influential talk-radio host, has been arguing that there is a 'narrow' alt-right made up of a 'execrable anti-Semitic, white supremacist fringe' but also a 'broad alt-right' made up of frustrated tea partiers and others who are simply hostile to the GOP establishment and any form of immigration reform that falls short of mass deportation. This isn't just wrong, it's madness. The alt-righters are a politically insignificant band. Why claim that a group dedicated to overthrowing conservatism for a white-nationalist fantasy is in fact a member of the conservative coalition? Why muddy a distinction the alt-righters are eager to keep clear?" Jonah Goldberg, "Time to John Birch the Alt-Right," *National Review*, August 31, 2016, http://www.nationalreview.com/article/439522/hillary-clinton-alt-right-conservatives-are-not-true-republicans.
26. Specifically, he said, "Me: Upon research, I noticed Jewish people run 95% of American media that is very interesting. Internet: Why do you want to gas the Jews?" Lukas Mikelionis, "Alt-Right Meltdown After Tweets About 'Jewish Question,'" *Heat Street*, December 27, 2016, http://heatst.com/culture-wars/alt-right-meltdown-after-tweets-about-the-jewish-question/.
27. Ibid.
28. For example, see Andrew Anglin, "Mike Cernovich, DeploraBall and the Collapse of the Alt-Cuck," *Daily Stormer*, December 28, 2016, http://www.dailystormer.com/mike-cernovich-deploraball-and-the-collapse-of-the-alt-cuck.

29. Rosie Gray, "The 'New Right' and the 'Alt-Right' Party on a Fractious Night," *Atlantic*, January 20, 2017, https://www.theatlantic.com/politics/archive/2017/01/the-new-right-and-the-alt-right-party-on-a-fractious-night/514001/.
30. Paul Joseph Watson, Twitter post, November 22, 2016, 1:45 p.m., https://twitter.com/PrisonPlanet/status/801179724768825345/photo/1.
31. Mike Cernovich, "CPAC—Big Crowds, Low Energy—It's Time for a New Right," *Danger and Play*, February 26, 2017, https://www.dangerandplay.com/2017/02/26/mike-cernovich-cpac-big-crowds-low-energy-heres-the-future-of-the-new-right/.
32. Richard A. Viguerie, *The New Right: We're Ready to Lead* (Falls Church, Va.: The Viguerie Company, 1980).
33. Charlie Nash, "MILO: White Nationalism Is Not the Answer," *Breitbart*, January 26, 2017, http://www.breitbart.com/milo/2017/01/26/milo-white-nationalism-is-not-the-answer/.
34. Loulla-Mae Eleftheriou-Smith, "Milo Yiannopoulos: Video of Right-Wing Journalist 'Defending Paedophilia' Surfaces Online," *Independent*, February 20, 2017, http://www.independent.co.uk/news/world/americas/milo-yiannopoulos-latest-news-paedophilia-breitbart-video-child-abuse-right-wing-sexual-relationship-a7589656.html.
35. "Breitbart News Hires from *The Hill*, *RealClearPolitics* in Latest Expansion," *Breitbart*, January 24, 2017, http://www.breitbart.com/big-journalism/2017/01/24/breitbart-news-hires-hill-realclearpolitics/.
36. Callum Borchers, "How Breitbart Could Lose Its Alt-Right Street Cred," *Washington Post*, January 25, 2017, https://www.washingtonpost.com/news/the-fix/wp/2017/01/25/how-breitbart-could-lose-its-alt-right-street-cred/.
37. Lawrence Murray, "Has the Alt-Lite Embraced the [North American] New Right?" *Atlantic Centurion*, January 5, 2017, https://atlanticcenturion.wordpress.com/2017/01/05/has-the-alt-lite-embraced-the-north-american-new-right/.

38. Éminence Grise, "Is the Dangerous Faggot Gone Yet?" *Right Stuff*, February 26, 2017, http://therightstuff.biz/2017/02/26/untitled-32/.

CONCLUSION

1. Brendan Karet, "Hillary Clinton's Speech on Trump's Alt-Right Support Highlights Right-Wing Media Fault Lines," *Media Matters for America*, August 25, 2016, http://mediamatters.org/research/2016/08/25/hillary-clinton-s-speech-trump-s-alt-right-support-highlights-right-wing-media-fault-lines/212678.
2. Milo Yiannopoulos, "FULL TEXT: 'How to Destroy the Alt-Right,'" *Breitbart*, September 19, 2016, http://www.breitbart.com/milo/2016/09/19/milo-destroy-alt-right-speech/.
3. Ibid.
4. Patricia Cartes, "Announcing the Twitter Trust & Safety Council," February 9, 2016, https://blog.twitter.com/2016/announcing-the-twitter-trust-safety-council.
5. Robert Tracinski, "#FreeStacy: The Old Regime and the Twitter Revolution," *Federalist*, February 22, 2016, http://thefederalist.com/2016/02/22/freestacy-the-old-regime-and-the-twitter-revolution/.
6. Allum Bokhari, "Twitter Declares War on Conservative Media, 'Unverifies' Breitbart Tech Editor Milo Yiannopoulos," *Breitbart*, January 9, 2016, http://www.breitbart.com/tech/2016/01/09/twitter-declares-war-on-conservative-media-unverifies-breitbart-tech-editor/.
7. Lucas Nolan, "Triggered: Ghostbusters Actress Leslie Jones Reports Milo to Twitter," *Breitbart*, July 18, 2016, http://www.breitbart.com/milo/2016/07/18/ghostbuster-leslie-jones-reports-milo/.
8. William Powers, "Who's Influencing Election 2016?" *MIT Media Lab*, February 23, 2016, https://medium.com/mit-media-lab/who-s-influencing-election-2016-8bed68ddecc3.

9. Travis M. Andrews, "'A Great Purge?': Twitter Suspends Richard Spencer, Other Prominent Alt-Right Accounts," *Washington Post*, November 16, 2016, https://www.washingtonpost.com/news/morning-mix/wp/2016/11/16/a-great-purge-twitter-suspends-richard-spencer-other-prominent-alt-right-accounts/.
10. Ibid.
11. Emma Grey Ellis, "Gab, the Alt-Right's Very Own Twitter, Is the Ultimate Filter Bubble," *Wired*, September 14, 2016, https://www.wired.com/2016/09/gab-alt-rights-twitter-ultimate-filter-bubble/.
12. David Frum, "Twitter's Misbegotten Censorship," *Atlantic*, November 16, 2016, http://www.theatlantic.com/politics/archive/2016/11/twitter-censorship-will-only-empower-the-alt-right/507929/.
13. Ibid.
14. Gideon Resnick, "Reddit Bans Alt-Right Group," *Daily Beast*, February 1, 2017, http://www.thedailybeast.com/articles/2017/02/01/reddit-bans-alt-right-group.html.
15. David Sherfinski, "Dan Schneider, ACU Executive Director, Denounces 'Alt-Right' Movement at CPAC," *Washington Times*, February 23, 2017, http://www.washingtontimes.com/news/2017/feb/23/dan-schneider-acu-executive-director-denounces-alt/.
16. Alan McEwen and Stephen Jones, "Racist Vlogger Who Became Global YouTube Sensation Unmasked as Jobless Ex-Student Who Lives with His Dad," *Daily Mirror*, January 9, 2017, http://www.mirror.co.uk/news/uk-news/racist-vlogger-who-became-global-9588308.
17. Jason Wilson, "Activists Claim to Unveil Leader of 'Alt-Right' Website *The Right Stuff*," *Guardian*, January 17, 2017, https://www.theguardian.com/world/2017/jan/17/right-stuff-alt-right-site-mike-enoch-revealed.
18. Ibid.
19. Matthew Sheffield, "The Alt-Right Eats Its Own: Neo-Nazi Podcaster 'Mike Enoch' Quits After Doxxers Reveal His Wife Is Jewish," *Salon*, January 16, 2017, http://www.salon.com/2017/01/16/cat-fight-on-the-alt-right-neo-nazi-podcaster-mike-enoch-quits-after-doxxers-reveal-his-wife-is-jewish/.

20. Richard Spencer, Twitter post, January 15, 2017, https://twitter.com/richardbspencer/status/820658999930535936.
21. Greg Johnson, "Why I Support Mike Enoch," *Counter-Currents*, January 17, 2017, http://www.counter-currents.com/2017/01/why-i-support-mike-enoch/print/.
22. Andrew Anglin, "Here's the Thing," *Daily Stormer*, January 15, 2017, http://www.dailystormer.com/heres-the-thing/.
23. Twitter direct message from Joshua Graham, February 13, 2017.
24. Southern Poverty Law Center, "Matthew Heimbach's Traditionalist Workers Party Was Confronted by Antifascist Organizations During a Protest in Sacramento, Calif., That Quickly Turned Violent," June 27, 2016, https://www.splcenter.org/hatewatch/2016/06/27/violent-clashes-erupt-sacramento-between-white-nationalists-and-antifascists.
25. Liam Stack, "Attack on Alt-Right Leader Has Internet Asking: Is It OK to Punch a Nazi?" *New York Times*, January 21, 2017, https://www.nytimes.com/2017/01/21/us/politics/richard-spencer-punched-attack.html.
26. David Weigel, "Milo Yiannopoulos Grabs Headlines in Wake of Berkeley Riot," *Washington Post*, February 3, 2017, https://www.washingtonpost.com/news/post-politics/wp/2017/02/03/milo-yiannopoulos-is-returning-to-white-house-briefing-room-in-wake-of-berkeley-riot/.
27. Jessica Chasmar, "Conservative Speaker Gavin McInnes Pepper-Sprayed by NYU Protesters," *Washington Times*, February 3, 2017, http://www.washingtontimes.com/news/2017/feb/3/gavin-mcinnes-conservative-speaker-pepper-sprayed-/.
28. Red Ice, "Richard Spencer from AltRight.com Talks About Being Sucker Punched by a Tolerant Leftie," *AltRight.com*, January 20, 2017, http://www.altright.com/2017/01/20/richard-spencer-from-altright-com-talks-about-being-sucker-punched-by-a-tolerant-leftie/.
29. Matt Parrot, "I'm Glad Richard Spencer Got Punched in the Face," *AltRight.com*, January 23, 2017, http://www.altright.com/2017/01/23/im-glad-richard-spencer-was-punched-in-the-face/.

30. Millennial Woes, "Is It Worth It? [speech to Identitarian Ideas IX, Stockholm]," YouTube Video, 16:22, posted February 26, 2017, https://www.youtube.com/watch?v=EbUJ_bUdDdU.
31. Rosie Gray, "A 'One-Stop Shop' for the Alt-Right," *Atlantic*, January 12, 2017, https://www.theatlantic.com/politics/archive/2017/01/a-one-stop-shop-for-the-alt-right/512921/.

INDEX

INDEX

INDEX

INDEX